ISSUE
DRIVEN
LIFE

ISSUE
DON'T LET IDIOTS
DRIVEN
RUIN YOUR DAY
LIFE

Elvin S. Ezekiel, Sr.

CITI OF BOOKS

CITIOFBOOKS, INC.
3736 Eubank NE Suite A1
Albuquerque, NM 87111-3579
www.citiofbooks.com
Hotline: 1 (877) 389-2759
Fax: 1 (505) 930-7244

Ordering Information:

Quantity sales. Special discounts are available on quantity purchases by corporations, associations, and others. For details, contact the publisher at the address above.

Printed in the United States of America.

ISBN-13:   Softcover   978-1-959682-97-4
               eBook   978-1-959682-98-1

Library of Congress Control Number: 2023904919

Dedicated to my lovely wife Lerma

Table of Contents

Prologue

For nearly fifty years I have conducted relational workshops, marriage seminars, conflict resolution studies, and addiction recovery throughout America and various parts of the world.

I understand clearly that people are simply acting out of who they are. People are often impacted by the pathology of their family systems and circumstances. There are those who practice various religious beliefs and creeds. However, they are simply people affected by experiences, tragedies, sometimes abuse, and other life-altering events. These occurrences on many occasions have reshaped thoughts and the ways of processing information. What is remarkable is that the conclusions that some come to have nothing to do with truth. Personal experiences shape perceptions. I personally do not believe that truth is relative.

You may not agree with the Christian paradigm however, as you read this material the enlightenment from the expressed dynamics will indeed bring you to understand and appreciate the horrors of being issue driven.

Stay with me until the end and experience the joy of understanding the people who make up your world. Some of you will look at others differently. You may even see in yourself practices that may hurt your preferred agenda.

I made learning about issues the business of my life; especially with regard to walking in a life of service. It is an area where I developed considerable expertise. I now advise people all over America and some parts of the world with regard to the issues that wreak havoc in their relationships, businesses, churches, and families.

This writing is not designed to replace medical advice. The analogies are all truthful and the stories have been modified to keep boundaries and to respect the privacy of those who are still being helped.

Please take a moment to relax and keep your mind open. The concepts in this writing may not be easily digestible for all. The word predisposition can be defined as a tendency to be held by condition, attitude, and a way of thinking or being. Some may be predisposed to fight a reality not consistent with their perception of their core belief. I choose to use "a way of thinking" to amplify or help explain the word predisposed. Instead of saying jack is predisposed to chaos, I will say the way Jack thinks or is thinking can be turbulent. This particular way of thinking can be very dangerous to one's sense of well-being. At the same time, one can be very comfortable and contented as the "thinker". People are embraced with their own thoughts and process things in their own way. Not necessarily logically or rationally. If you challenge them about the way they think or process you will meet with great opposition. Christians especially have to be careful about the enemy of progress and success is by definition "magical thinking". Magical thinking is a system of reasoning unique to a particular thinker. What they think and how they process makes perfect sense to them. Magical thinking by some Christians, embraces some scriptures, some logic, and very often someone else's experience to justify its position or perception. After these ingredients have been absorbed a predisposition (a way of thinking) now exists. Pure logic and truth are very often painful and difficult for the magical thinker to connect with. Let's look at the person who gambles addictively. These individuals very often are prisoners of the notion that they must risk it all to advance their cause (magical thinking). A man said to me once "I am praying that I hit the state lotto so that I can be a blessing to the church"

When gamblers are up by a little they still will not stop. Logic would say don't risk your gain. The person with the predisposition to gambling is not controlled or ruled by logic. There is a notion that rules his/her being. Here it is! They love the action, the juice. Living on the edge is exciting and appealing to their core. The fantasy to win and win it all drives the behavior. The predisposition (their way of thinking) fuels the fantasy and energizes the destructive behavior.

For the sake of this writing, we will identify the behavior and way of thinking in the previous analogy as "addictive or issue driven".

Introduction

Some wonder why people of renown become troubled or trapped by embarrassing circumstances. My response is why not. People are just people, even the ones we hold in high regard. Because of the tenacity of news reporters, we become aware of the behaviors of some public figures. The sexual allegations against Donald Trump, U S Senators Franken and Moor, Anthony Weiner, Tiger Woods, former President Bill Clinton, and former Presidential Candidate John Edwards have purported issues with infidelity. John Michael Farren, former General Counsel at the Xerox Corporation and Deputy Counsel to former President George H.W. Bush, has issues with his temper (I call it rage-a-holism). It was reported (I read it on Aol.com) that he beat his wife with a metal flashlight and attempted to strangle her for delivering divorce papers. She stated, "She could not deal with his explosive temper." We know this now because of what we read or hear. We very often do not understand why. It is perplexing to observe the quagmire of some of the events that well known people and our heroes are stuck with. It is not necessarily, what they are stuck in but what they are stuck with. A loosely but often used term is "issues." It is disturbing that so many people carry the baggage of destructive issues. Like a baseball driven out of the ballpark by a tremendous swing of the bat, so are the individuals that are possessed with destructive issues. These issues drive men and women into infidelity, drug abuse, overeating, and rage just to name a few. Issues can cause people to tell lies, cheat, overspend, and mismanage their life's resources. Many Americans suffer from the influence of issues on their behavior and choices and have no idea what is driving them. This dynamic is not limited to the color of your skin, social status, or intellectual acumen.

Issues can be a part of anyone's life, and affect all relationships and one's destiny. Issues have no respect for popularity or political persuasion.

Multiple sex partners could be an indicator of being issue driven. People with multiple partners can mean that one is objectifying people and reducing them to merely objects of pleasure. Very Often, Issue driven people have no concern about wounds and damage caused by their selfishness and insensitivity.

America has become the nation of the obese. Overeating is a pandemic with no relief in view. People eat to numb their pain; I talked to someone who ate to remove themselves from the dating cycle because they very often are afraid of rejection. Others have learned to eat because of the modeling by their chief caregivers. Thus, they eat because it is an issue, not necessarily because they are hungry, but because there is an unmet emotional need.

Most people have some issues. The need to examine and work on them is paramount. An issue driven life is just that. It is not a life led by purpose and resolve but driven by issues. If one is not careful, the issue becomes the purpose.

Chapter 1

Purpose versus Issue

However, some people have written purposes but their issues hijack the effort.

One day I was in my office weeping and meditating about the upheaval in my family. It was a very difficult time, so I thought to go to my church office and spend some quiet time with God. One of the members of my church walked in while I was oblivious to any sounds. I frankly was uninterested in greeting or having a dialogue with anyone. After seeing an unfamiliar look on my face this person sheepishly walked away. I was having a very personal and private experience at that time. During that moment, I refused interruption.

A while later, that member came to me and asked, "If I was angry with her?" Caught off guard I was Shocked, I said "no of course not!" She intimated to me that her abandonment issues were kicking up and she needed to ask me to be sure that it was not her fault. I was in a state, but it was not her doing. However, my unwillingness to engage in a conversation triggered a memory of her "being abandoned." This happens so often. There are many experiences that trigger the recollection of past memories and hurts.

This person was extremely troubled by her past. She made the decision that she wanted more for her life and began working on her issues. However, she was a long way from the finish line of a healthy perspective, but honest enough to not walk away with her own thoughts

1

being the bottom line. I commended her for the resolve to ask her own self-tough questions. Issue driven people do the opposite; they walk away being their own bottom line. If you challenge them, you will meet with much resistance and sometimes hostility.

Should we explore more closely the dynamic of the conversation between my church member and me, the term projection would be an accurate description or label. I often am involved with family systems where projections are the chosen mode of communication. These individuals do not really hear what you say or mean. They simply *project* their feelings into the mix and hold those feelings to be what you mean or meant. It becomes very difficult to help or communicate with individuals prone to this kind of behavior.

Ponder for a moment the complexity of the issue driven. You make a statement or ask a question. The person responds according to their feelings and issues. Your question is simply a reminder (a trigger) of their feelings or experience of being attacked. Memories of another day, these memories are not precious.

Issue driven behavior is very common in America and almost every other country in the world. It would be wonderful if we all could be purpose driven or live **"The Purpose Driven Life"** as written by Rick Warren. I think personally that his writing helped people in a very positive way. However, some people have written purposes but their issues hijack the effort. If it were that easy, they simply would make a plan to achieve a desired goal and go for it. This is not the case with many people; there is a predisposition or tendency to hurt ourselves or situations. To clarify, the dictionary states with regard to predisposition, "increased vulnerability to a particular behavior.... based on certain underlying conditions not yet active or revealed." Another dictionary, "Wikipedia" suggests an inclination or willingness.

Some unfortunate people are born with health issues. The road that they must travel is very different. For the sake of this writing, we will explore the issues of the inner person and its effect. This is not an attempt to be exhaustive but to raise awareness of issues among the unsuspecting. Issues are just an inclination to be, think, or act a certain way. Logic, reasonableness, and protocols are not often in the thoughts of issue driven people. These people because of their issues choose to understand what they hear through their own skewed feelings and emotions. This is not done maliciously; often it is subconscious mechanisms at work. Some are defensive others may be offensive. Connecting with these people can be difficult. Over half of the marriages in America end in divorce mainly because of this dynamic, "issue driven behavior." It may not be *projection* as mentioned earlier; it may be one of many dysfunctional behaviors. They are nonetheless "issue driven."

Purpose is the intent or motive behind a selected action. Ideally, (1) we make decisions to fulfill a purpose; (2) we identify the purpose or goal; and (3) we then go for it. A purpose driven life is one guided or propelled by the selected purpose. We measure where we are by nearness to completion. People with issues may write goals. They may even start the journey with some success. Personal issues in one's life can work against desired purposes or goals. By nature, these negative issues are self-sabotaging and self-destructive.

To clarify, if you like a clean house and you work hard to keep it clean this is not an issue. If you are cleaning every hour throughout the day or most days, this may be an issue. If you go somewhere and can hardly contain yourself over the appearance or look of the home of someone else, you have an issue. If you often tend to suggest to other people how they should keep their homes, you probably have some control issues. It may be your purpose to keep your home neat for your family; this is a good thing, and it is admirable. However, you may be issue driven when violating the boundaries of others, by telling them what to do in their own homes. The same may be true when telling others how to live if the advice is unsolicited.

Learning what issues are is important. Learning what issues you have is essential. Issues unattended and not resolved tend to take over our lives. We cannot defeat an unknown enemy. We cannot fight what we do not see. Issues are like a field of buried bombs (land mines). It is hard to know where you can walk. Purposes may be written and stated; however, issues can drive us the other way. Issues can and will destroy marriages, a ministry, effectiveness, and many other endeavors. Thus, we live with frustration and pain.

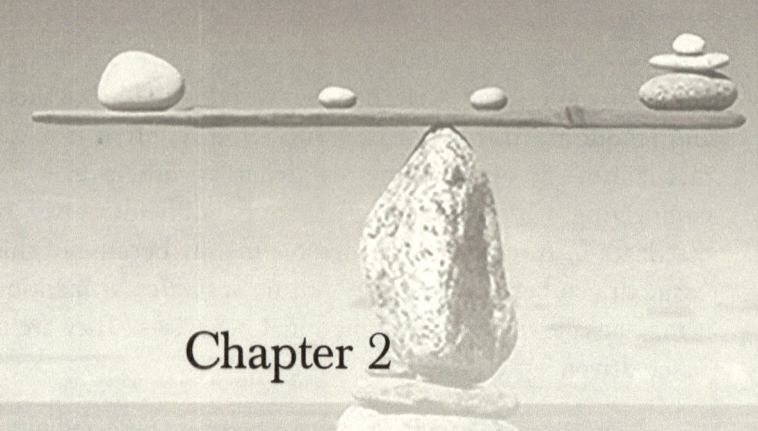

Chapter 2

You can't make others love you

She was incapable and unwilling to love because of her issues.

Henry was a pretty good photographer. He made his money by doing weddings, proms, and children's parties. He earned a comfortable living. At one of his pre-wedding functions, he met a pretty young woman. What he did not know initially was that she was the bride-to-be. He loved the attention he was getting from her. He felt uncommonly validated.

The groom (now husband) called me six months after the wedding asking for advice. He was complaining about the lack of harmony in the marriage. He could not understand her lack of affection. Counseling did not work for this couple. The wife came to my office later and confessed to me that she had been in an affair with Henry the photographer.

After the breakup of the marriage, Dina began to live with Henry. Henry's great disappointment was that the relationship failed miserably.

Dina was not a mean person however, she was extremely needy. She really wanted to be happy and only knew how to survive on attention. Her looks gave her the opportunity to be very often admired and desired. Twenty years later Dina is still needy, unhappy, and unmarried. The husband incorrectly thought that he could cause Dina to love him. Henry the photographer fell into the same trap and failed as well. She was incapable and unwilling to love because of her issues.

Like many issue driven people, her low self-esteem drove Dina into a behavior pattern that could only temporarily keep a relationship going. With disturbing issues like Dina, one would be wise to face the reality of a failed agenda. When one is inundated with low self-esteem, he or she must find a counselor or support group. In those sessions, one will discover their sense of worth and value. To my knowledge, Dina never has moved past her dependence on looks and flirty tactics. These are some superficial tools used by the shallow. Shallow people erroneously believe that with such tools they can inspire love. Proverbs 3:5 (NIV) Trust in the Lord with all your heart and lean not on your own understanding.

Chapter 3

Jane's Story

The addict is addicted to the substance or behavior; the codependent is addicted to the addict.

Jane's purpose was to be a good and caring mother. Like so many others she was a single parent. She would not delegate the task of taking care of her children to another. Raising her two sons by herself was a great challenge. She spared no pain and gave everything she could to provide for her boys. Edward, the oldest, learned very early to help his mother and made life as easy as he could for her. Timothy, the youngest, never developed the same tendencies as his brother. There was not that much to do in the home, his mother and brother did everything except clean his room. When young Timothy became a teenager, he began to experiment with drugs. Although his mother was upset she continued to do her very best, she sacrificed herself for both boys. Edward graduated from college and married a young church girl. Timothy just drifted through life never really accomplishing anything. He enjoyed life on the streets. He became addicted to the "so-called" fast life as well as the drugs he sold and used. He became his best customer. Jane tried everything to get her son to stop abusing drugs and living the life of an unbeliever. He would often steal from her and it would break her heart. She would forgive him every time, for she believed this to be her God-given burden to bear. She was often urging her older son to go get his brother and bring him back to her. Edward believed that Timothy made his choice and he would have to live with the consequences. Edward was like his mother in that he saved and provided well for his family. Timothy was a taker and user. He knew what he was doing was wrong but his issues would not let him go. He could not bring himself to care past his own perceived need.

Jane died after a long illness. She left a will, which gave the two sons what was left of her estate Much had been squandered by her younger son's life style. To Edward, she left $20,000 and to Timothy, she left the house that she raised them in and $60,000. She stated in her will "Timothy needed more," so she left him the majority of her estate.

Codependency, in nonprofessionals terms can be defined as: someone connected in a relationship in which one person is psychologically dependent in an unhealthy way on someone who is addicted to a substance or self-destructive behavior. Jane died never understanding what codependency means or how it works. The addict is addicted to the substance or behavior; the codependent is addicted to the addict. We define addiction as behavior committed at the expense of one's belief system. Codependency feels like love, however, it is very enabling. The codependent experiences feelings of protection for the addict. They want to give the addict another chance. This so-called "help", enables the addict to stay addicted even if you the codependent do not want to do so. Addicts cannot survive without a codependent or in other words a co-addict. To be clear the codependent is an addict as well. Most codependents see themselves as mercy givers. They believe themselves to be filled with compassion and the love of God. When in actuality they are enabling or helping the addict to stay on their own self-destructive path.

Within three months, Timothy spent the $60,000 he inherited from his mother on drugs and sold the house not long after for a pittance. Jane died as she lived being codependent on her youngest son. She was a good person embraced by an addiction that felt like love. She was an issue driven as was her son Timothy.

The unpleasant and stark reality is that Jane died as an addict while enabling Timothy to be one. This is not a unique story it is being played out all over our country and the world by the issue driven.

Love operates very differently. Love does what is best; it cannot do what only feels good. Sometimes love has to be tough and say no. Sometimes the Lover must separate him/herself from the addict or issue driven individual. Love itself has no limits, however, there should be limitations to what love will tolerate. If loving you means that I cannot love myself something is definitely wrong. If by loving you I cannot provide for myself and my responsibilities, then this is not love but codependency. I as a Christian must give an account of my stewardship. God is looking for an increase in his investment in our lives. Again, we conclude that codependency is a driving issue. Romans 7:19 (World English Bible) For the good which I desire, I don't do; which I don't desire, but the evil which I don't desire, I practice.

Chapter 4

Shaniqua's story

Shameless behavior leads to shame-based behavior in children. These children grow up to be adults controlled by guilt and shaming.

Shaniqua was born in the ghetto of a northeastern city. Her mother was a drug addict and her father was unknown to her. She was raised in poverty and with no supervision. Her mother spent all of her time hustling for drugs. When Shaniqua turned eleven her mother viewed her body development as an opportunity. Shaniqua was evolving quickly into a young lady, so her mother sold her for money to get high. Any guy who had a penchant for young girls would do. Shaniqua went kicking and screaming eventually she learned to comply. Her mother rationalized that her daughter had to do her part to keep the family going.

Whenever a parent operates without shame and in an inappropriate way, it is labeled shameless behavior. Shameless behavior leads to shame-based behavior in children. These children grow up to be adults controlled by guilt and shaming.

We will fast forward to Shaniqua's adulthood. With her boundaries very often violated in her youth and no father in her life to developing balance, she has the tendency to be attracted to men who are emotionally unavailable. She is working on her third marriage. Her son of a previous relationship is a low achiever even in the face of his mother's climb upward in the prison correctional system. When talking to her she exhibits extreme bitterness toward her mother who is living now on the streets.

Because of the chaos in Shaniqua's early life she overcompensated, and she is now a very controlling person. It worked well for her as a correctional officer. It is counterproductive with regard to raising her son, and her involvement in romantic relationships. Shaniqua is not a bad person and she is helpful to people around her.

She did not ask for the hand that was dealt her. However, issue driven family systems can be ruthless and volatile. The issue driven family system can push people into lifestyles and behaviors that are very edgy. The Jekyll and Hide syndrome is not an uncommon dynamic in issue driven lives.

Chapter 5

Relationship issues

What they very often do not see is that they have idolized the notion of being connected with the other person rather than discover the other person's core..

Managing relationships is one of the most important elements in the Christian life. The nature of our relationships is reflective of our relationship with the God. Countless groups of people wrongly believe that a viable relationship with God can exist exclusive of a connection with people and their issues. Christian instruction teaches that one cannot jump over people and get to God. Relationships become a major measuring device with regard to how aligned we are with the principles of our Creator.

Maintaining relationships requires a great deal of effort. Relationships do not remain intact automatically. The establishment of boundaries is one of the most important elements in relationships. Respecting and understanding the limits of another person is far more essential than most realize. Knowledge of where one individual starts and stops clearly defines the groundwork for healthy involvement. Enmeshed relationships are "control-ships" states Vince Depasqualle of the "*Starting Point*" in Westmont, New Jersey. The book of Corinthians in the bible tells us to "commend ourselves to every man's conscience in the sight of God." All of us have differences and those differences need to be respected.

Healthy Relationships help keep us accountable and balanced. Without them, we often become our own bottom line.

Issue driven people are difficult to connect with in relationships. The "issue driven" often filled with fears, is extremely uncomfortable with actions, words, and behaviors that expose them. They would rather fight than switch. One must stroke their egos to get along and never openly challenge or call them on behaviors that may be inappropriate. Issue driven people can be volatile and combative. When their core issues are being touched and exposed they tend to deflect. Truth is not always the friend of the issue driven.

Issue driven men and women who are Christians meet in hope of a Godly and happy marriage relationship. What they very often do not see is that they have idolized the notion of being connected with the other person rather than discovering the other person's core. Later they become very angry feeling betrayed and let down. The home they created is filled with tension and stress. God help the children raised in this place of conflicting signals and mercurial emotions.

What are our options? Should we just abdicate or quit? I say no! Fight for the healthy. You should not deliberately antagonize however, allowing issues to rule the relationship creates a dysfunctional home and environment. Counseling and accountability are essential for healing. Make no mistake the issue driven are wounded and hurting. Hurting people tend to hurt people. Hurting people is very difficult to be intimate with. They cannot risk sharing their inner selves without feeling threatened. The complexity of their guilt, shame, and fear creates such a barrier to intimate relationships. What comes from them can be insensitive and callous. Some have learned to mask their issues by deflective actions. Without realizing it they build walls that separate not bridges that connect. Proverbs 14:12 (KJV) There is a way that which seemeth right unto a man, but the end thereof are the ways of death. This means death to your effectiveness, death to your dreams, death to your productivity, and death to your relationships.

Chapter 6

One way connections

The denial is so entrenched that no other reality can penetrate

Very often we find ourselves in relationships that are one-sided. By this I am defining involvements where one person does most of the caring, validating, and nurturing. It can be exasperating to be the one doing all the giving.

During my nearly 30- years of ministry, there have been many milestones to mark the years. I thank God for the many positive and rewarding events in my life. Unfortunately, there were other times, which were not my proudest moments. Not only did I fail God during these turbulent and dark times, but also I am painfully aware that I was the cause of hurt and pain for many people. As a believer committed to the principles set forth in the Scriptures, I take every opportunity to "*repair the breach.*" According to the "recovery" paradigm, we are responsible for our actions and thus we must make amends to the people we have mistreated or offended.

With regard to the hurt we have caused others, we must recognize that the mere utterance of "I am sorry" may not be enough. These words are not created from Biblical principles; rather, the Biblical paradigm requires godly sorrow followed by repentance for our wrongdoing. Too often, the words "I am sorry" are simply a phrase of convenience used by humans to help them feel better about their actions. By not naming our specific transgressions, we are not taking full responsibility for how we have hurt others. Brokenness and contriteness are prerequisites for reconciliation. However, our ability to attain this healthy attitude directly hinges on our intentional willingness to specifically identify and confess our negative`` actions and behaviors. During the presidential campaign, candidate Donald Trump chooses to give a blanket apology without specifics. Christians are challenged to be spiritually aligned. However, many are only politically correct. The standard for acceptable behavior is in the word of God, not the rhetorical nonsense given in the spin room of a political campaign.

When we have caused pain we must become willing to hear and bear the painful expressions of the ones we injured.

I hope this writing presents a challenge that will enable you to travel on the road to reconciliation. Restoration in all your relationships; especially those in which you were chiefly responsible for the injury, is essential. Be very careful that in your efforts to reconcile you are not looking for cheap seats, or in other words doing that, that costs the least. To allow confrontation and to seek the forgiveness of others is far more pleasing to God than choosing the path that costs nothing.

Many people simply offer a general apology, not really targeting the point of the offense or pain. To be truly sorry requires more than words. Do you have pride or some other issue that sabotages a genuine need to make up? Marriages and other needful relationships remain torn because of the issues we harbor in our being. Those broken by the conviction of the Holy Spirit seek more than a casual reconnection. They are willing to do all in order to reconcile.

God's desire to have a reconciled relationship with His creation cost Him very much, the earthly assassination of Jesus. The Son of God came from heaven and humbled himself even to death on the cross. There has never been a greater act of humility or love.

If God is willing to come down and become man to be humiliated and cursed by men, what is our problem that we can't come down and apologize? I will tell you "Issue Driven".

We must build healthy and happy relationships. It is a challenge to do so. Relationships are not automatic. The enemy of our soul comes to "rob, steal, and destroy." The disruption of family harmony is the goal of the unrighteous. Invest your time in a healthy manner with consideration of boundaries and commending yourselves to one another's feelings. John 10:10 (KJV) the thief comes only to steal, and kill and destroy.....

There is a sad reality that some people have reached a tipping point in their dysfunctional behavior. They lived too long without working or seeing their self. The denial is so entrenched that no other reality can penetrate. Trying to challenge these people into having a more reciprocated exchange of feelings and ideas is almost an exercise of futility.

We are challenged by our Lord to love them; however, we are not required to let them walk over our feelings as though we do not exist.

Chapter 7

Control Issues

I will state this clearly and emphatically, unsolicited advice is controlling!

I ndividuals with control issues have trouble with boundaries, often thinking that their unsolicited advice and opinions are in the best interest of the advisee. Issue driven controllers will always use some kind of rationalization or justification as to why they cross boundaries. Often you hear it said, "It is for their good." It is never okay for any individual to play God. No one needs anyone else to make decisions for him or her. God's word clearly explains that He weighs the intent of the heart. God will not judge me based on your agenda. The controlling person does his/her so-called "good deeds" not for the person, but for the agenda of the controller. Giving "good advice" to those who "need it" validates the advisor. This kind of controlling behavior gives them a sense of worth and well-being. The boundaries of the needy are never a concern for the controlling person.

Miranda was molested by her stepfather. No one in her large family believed her. Her accusations served to dishonor the polished image that her mother fought to maintain. The mother of Miranda became extremely irritated with her. Life was not pleasant in the home of her origin.

She did not understand the impact that the chaos of her youth would have in her adult life. She is very intelligent. She became a follower Of Jesus and she loved God very much. However, her damaged boundaries enabled her to be unfaithful in her marriage. She became sexually involved with her pastor who was also in a bad marriage. They both believed that they had a special understanding of each other. Miranda felt that she could be happy with her pastor if they were both free. They broke off the illicit part of their involvement and moved on with their lives. When Miranda found out that her pastor was involved with someone close to her she became enraged. Then, feeling like a victim she became bitter and attempted to rectify all of the wrongs and indiscretions around her. She became a crusader with opinions about everyone and everything.

She deflected the notion that she too might share in the responsibility of her affair. She knew that she was married and involved with a married man. However, the hurt and sense of betrayal she experienced pushed her into a more ungodly attitude of self-righteousness. Proverb 18:12 (NIV) Before a downfall the heart is haughty, but humility comes before honor.

Controlling people typically refuse to humble themselves. The chaos of Miranda's past youth coupled with her self-inflicted wounds produced an unwillingness to trust. She has fared well professionally however; her personal life has not been fruitful. She has opinions that are strong and tilted toward her created reality. She does connect with the other controlling individuals in her family and circle. These people were damaged by the same family system that sired Miranda's predisposition.

Controlling people will decide what is best for the individuals around them. They arrange and manipulate. The church world is full of people who engineer relationships and events for the sake of their own agendas. Later they may label it God's will.

I will state this clearly and emphatically, unsolicited advice is controlling!

Chapter 8

Mabel's Story

The relational system designed by Mabel's issues requires her daughter to be a screw-up so that Mabel will have to instruct her.

Mabel married early in life. The man she chose to marry was emotionally unavailable. She was his trophy. He was uncaring, insensitive, and a braggart. She believed that she had affairs with other men because of the missing ingredients in her marriage. She was unaware that her past had affected her (her dad was not present during her developing years). All of the men she was attracted to on the surface were great guys. However, they all were emotionally unavailable. In most cases, an affair with a married person is an attraction to the unavailable, for they too are involved with someone else. There is not enough time to be around everyone so they spread themselves thin. The married partner with the extra-curricular friend can only give so much.

Mabel's marriage produced no children. Near the end of the marriage and after numerous affairs with other men, she became pregnant by a lover. She raised the child by herself. Mabel was awesome in her diligence to provide the best for her darling daughter. Nothing was too good for her child. Mabel never found relational bliss. Nevertheless, she was never without a man, she continued to search hoping to land the right person.

Mabel is and was very controlling. Her relationships with men never last long. She was always telling her daughter what to do even in the most insignificant matters. Her daughter has low self-esteem. Her daughter did not develop a sense of self-worth. That is what happens when being under the influence of an overwhelming parent. Later Mabel perceived her daughter to be rebellious and defiant. In actuality, her daughter was subconsciously trained by Mabel to never trust herself or see her own decisions as adequate. When her daughter became promiscuous, Mabel blamed it on the absence of the father in the child's life. The Daughter continues to pick men in defiance of her mother's rules. The relational system designed by Mabel's issues requires her daughter to be a screw-up so that Mabel will have to instruct her. Ironically the cycle of abuse in the family continues. The controlling behavior modeled by Mabel was later embraced by the daughter.

Mabel is a successful person by the world's standards. However, her family and friends quietly speak of her overbearing ways. Some suggest that Mabel was simply unlucky in love. She however tends to be very intense with her passive-aggressive conduct. Most men will not tolerate it. All relationships with Mabel are on her terms or they are not going to last. I spoke with Mabel on many occasions she does not see herself.

There are many ways that control issues can be manifested some start out with very noble intentions. However, well-meaning does not mitigate itself against the principle. God made us all and our individuality is to be respected and regarded, even if you have a better idea. (KJV) 2 Corinthians 4:2 But have renounced the hidden things of dishonesty, not walking in craftiness, nor handling the word of God deceitfully, but by the manifestation of the truth commending ourselves to every man's conscience in the sight of God.

Chapter 9

The Controlling Pastor

Denial is a skill we learn as children to insulate us from the pain of reality.

Pastor K. and his wife are wonderful people, in as much as he would give you the shirt off his back. Pastor K. is conscientious about God and is always looking to share the good news. Pastor K. comes from a dysfunctional family. His mother had low self-esteem and was the victim of abusive men. Pastor K. lost his father at a young age. When pastor K. began his ministry, it was amazing to see his church grow with so many young people. After some time the young people did what young people often do, they became sexually involved with each other in the ministry. Concerned and alarmed, Pastor K. prayed and came up with a solution. The pastor with his considerable influence suggested very strongly that certain leading young people should marry. He chose mates among the group. This matchmaking was done with acceptance by the group because Pastor K. had the wisdom and "heard from God." However, none of those marriages became successful relationships. It was years later before this dynamic became public. The children of these marriages became even more dysfunctional than the parents; their lives were also issue driven. There was no place for discussion of the inner struggles of the parents with their children.

The parents felt guilty and ashamed as they raised their children, although they believed they should be happy. In addition, because their marriages did not work, they believed that they had failed God. The congregation became shameful bases on its core value system. The ministry became cultish in its operation and procedures. A leader among the older attendees often sold to the congregation, how wonderful Pastor K. was and is. There was no accountability but tons of underlying pain was never revealed or expressed openly. However, the repressed pain of many erupted in other ways. The issues that developed among the group are only indicative of the greater problem. However, as many dysfunctional people do, they dealt with the surface issues as if they were the problem. Very often issues are an indicator. Attempting to resolve the superficial is like putting the cart before the horse.

Joining people together in marriage, with no compatibility or common interests created such horror in many lives. The domino effect is still wreaking havoc today even with families long gone from the church ministry. The ministry of Pastor K. is issue driven. Fear and guilt kept many of these couples together and prevented them from leaving Pastor K.'s church. Anyone who leaves the ministry because they could not take the controlling methodology of Pastor K or his theological position that justified his every move is labeled unfavorably. Leaving for almost any reason was never appreciated. They are viewed as spiritually inept. Controlling pastors work this way, fostering negative views of departing individuals. To leave, one feels disloyal to "God's will." Personal goals and ambitions must take a back seat to the controller's agenda.

I want to make it clear that with many people, being issue driven results in critical selfishness and self-absorbed behavior. Issue driven individuals too often hurt others and are insensitive to the pain caused by their issue driven activity. Pastor K. is controlling even if his intent was to help and not harm. Nonetheless, he and his wife are the authors of pain. {I include his wife} A public apology would do wonders for the fallen and wounded. However, an apology is admitting that his life's work has been for naught. Denial is a skill we often learn as children to insulate us from the pain of reality. "Issue driven" lives exist because of denial. An individual with real substance in his/her character has elements of humility. They can, and do come down. They learned to own their "stuff." It is difficult to build relationships with people in denial.

Pastor K has gotten older. The congregation has dwindled significantly, however; his controlling tendencies have not diminished.

Chapter 10

Eating

All issues are self-destructive; learning to love ourselves is the only antidote.

Eating is a normal function. However, issues of overeating can be a driving element with various complexities. The over-eater does food the same way the drug addict does drugs. The issue driven eater is attempting to numb him/herself from some kind of inner pain. However, the guilt of overeating causes more pain and the cycle continues. Unfortunately, the overeater seldom is able to hide the result of their overeating. The weight gain becomes remarkable accompanied by rationalizations. The already lowered self-esteem plummets even more.

Alison was abandoned by her mother at an early age. Father was a very successful businessman who drank all the time. Alison received no nurturing from her father. Left to herself she began to comfort herself with food and all kinds of snacks.

My involvement began when Alison while in college. At this time she was morbidly obese. The doctors suggested gastrointestinal bypass surgery to save her life. Even after the surgery, her mindset was still as an overeater. She never got over her abandonment issues and food became her best friend. As bright and intelligent as she was, her emotional predisposition continued to spiral downward. Not uncommon with addicts she was cross-addicted. Meaning she became compelled to drink and have affairs with married men. Why married men one may ask? The answer is simple married men are emotionally unavailable. She replicated her earlier childhood by being involved with someone who would not be there for her need of self-being and self-worth. She was attracted to people who would leave, and duplicate the pain of the absence of her father emotionally.

All issues are self-destructive; learning to love ourselves is the only antidote. When we love ourselves we begin to want what is best for us versus what is good for us.

If one becomes involved in a personal relationship with a significant other while still practicing self-destruction it most definitely will make life more difficult. Unfortunately the self-destructive are driven to operate involvements in a counterproductive way.

Marriage was designed by God to de-centralize us.

With regard to the topic of marriage I will echo briefly some general concerns however, I am compelled to speak also about divorce. Idiots (later to be explained) will contrive some justification with regard to divorce. God did not design divorce as an escape from convenience. It is not supposed to be a relief for those who are simply too selfish, too self-absorbed, and too self-centered to work on or through relational difficulties.

Mature individuals do not enter into a marriage based solely on emotions and feelings. Unfortunately, many people do. This in fact speaks loudly of their immaturity. In particular, issue driven involvements push others to the edge and then some. Of those who wish to have a God-centered relationship, they should abstain from sexual involvement prior to marriage, choosing rather work out differences without the drug of sex and remain sober. If individuals love God they are indeed concerned with honoring His word with a heart of obedience. When a couple chooses to be together for six to nine months and work through their personality and character challenges without the experience of sexual activity, they gain a tremendous advantage over their sexually active counterparts. Those abstaining from their driving passions are guaranteeing themselves to have a healthier and more prosperous marriage. It is simply idiotic to transgress God's law and look to have the best outcome.

Marriage was designed by God to de-centralize us. Living with another personality and character is essential to spiritual development. Sacrificing our needs and wants for the sake of someone else is Christ-like. Becoming godly is the goal of the Creator for everyone. Marriage done right and approached with the biblical mandate will produce people who learn to be concerned with the feelings and needs of others. Marriages of convenience are not so productive. They should read the book of 1st Corinthians 13. The chief agenda of our Lord is love and loving. Love should be unconditional. Real love is kind and long-suffering. When individuals embrace biblical concepts of love they become better people and productive citizens.

There are no born lovers. When love is properly modeled in a home by parents who love unconditionally, the children have a better chance of having an issue-less life. The home is the institution where values and principles should be taught and embraced. Children growing up observing mom and dad considering one another develop a better sense of self and healthy perspectives.

Because some hearts hate being challenged they are beyond receiving help, divorce then is an unavoidable evil with consequences. A very large percentage of children from divorced homes, in their adult lives, become divorced.

Consequently, the pain of separation and divorce creates an issue that is in all likelihood self-destructive. We must remember the principle given in the beginning everything brings forth after its own kind.

Chapter 11

Marriage

<u>Marriage was designed by God to de-centralize us</u>

With regard to the topic of marriage I will echo briefly about some general concerns however, I am compelled to speak also about divorce. Idiots (later to be explained) will contrive some justification with regard to divorce. God did not design divorce as an escape of convenience. It is not supposed to be relief for those who are simply too selfish, too self-absorbed, and too self-centered to work on or through relational difficulties.

Mature individuals do not to enter into marriage based solely on emotions and feelings. Unfortunately many people do. This in fact speaks loudly of their immaturity. In particular, issue driven involvements push others to the edge and then some. Of those whom wish to have a God centered relationship, they should abstain from sexual involvement prior to marriage, choosing rather to work out differences without the drug of sex and remain sober. If individuals love God they are indeed concerned with honoring His word with a heart of obedience. When a couple chooses to be together for six to nine months and work through their personality and character challenges without the experience of sexual activity, they gain a tremendous advantage over their sexually active counterparts. Those abstaining from their driving passions are guaranteeing themselves to have a healthier and more prosperous marriage. It is simply idiotic to transgress God's law and look to have the best outcome.

Marriage was designed by God to de-centralize us. Living with another personality and character is essential to spiritual development. Sacrificing our needs and wants for the sake of someone else is Christ-like. Becoming godly is the goal of the Creator for everyone. Marriage done right and approached with the biblical mandate will produce people who learn to be concerned with the feelings and needs of others. Marriages of convenience are not so productive. They should read the book of 1st Corinthians 13. The chief agenda of our Lord is love and loving. Love should be unconditional. Real love is kind and long suffering. When individual embrace biblical concepts of love they become better people and productive citizens.

There are no born lovers. When love is properly modeled in a home by parents who love unconditionally, the children have a better chance of having an issue-less life. The home is the institution where values and principles should be taught and embraced. Children growing up observing mom and dad considering one another develop a better sense of self and healthy perspectives.

Because some hearts hate being challenged they are beyond receiving help, divorce then is an unavoidable evil with consequences. A very large percent of children from divorced homes, in their adult lives, become divorced.

Consequently the pain of separation and divorce create an issue that is in all likelihood self-destructive. We must remember the principle given in the beginning everything bringing forth after its own kind.

Chapter 12

Issue Driven Managers

They attempt to mask their ugliness. Unfortunately, not everyone around them is blind.

I worked in corporate America as an implementation consultant. I started out teaching software implementation and now I do a leadership development, conflict resolution, and sensitivity training. My niche is my ability to assess the needs of the people I am working with and meet them at the point of their needs. This in turn helps them neutralize potential blow-ups. Very often, I meet people in management positions with major internal conflicts. This is a proactive way of saying "they have issues." Many are not aware of the issues that affect them and the people they manage. "Relationship building" is the key to the proper management of people. To determine accurately the proper course of action and to move forward one must have the ability to listen. This will separate the best from the rest.

However, issue driven people have a skewed sense of reality. They do not see things as they are, but rather as they perceive them to be. Many issue driven managers listen to the communication of people through their own unproductive filters. They are not hearing the heart of the matter, they are listening to their own perceptions, and too often they are projecting. Obviously, poor listening skills hurt the overall effort. This then affects morale and ultimately throws the team into mediocrity or even chaos. Poor decision-making hurts productivity in the end.

Effective and productive managers tend to be honest with themselves and stay aware of their limitations and potentially dangerous issues. Irresponsible people are continuously afraid; their fear of exposure is a primary concern and very painful. The issue driven manager may lead by pushing the buttons of those under him/her. Keeping their subordinates off balance is sometimes an unspoken joy. Their denial is firmly entrenched to protect them from reality. Looking good is an enormously driving issue with them. They attempt to mask their ugliness. Unfortunately, not everyone around them is blind. It is tragic that careers and life resources are in the hands of these issue driven people.

Donald is an extremely warm and vibrant person. He has a great personality and as a course, he makes everyone around him feel better. He manages with a sense of purpose and he is a great team leader. Everyone likes him. However, Donald's sexual issues have plagued him all of his adult life. Early he thought that this is what "guys" do (The American myth). Later he read and discovered a particular truth about himself, the sex he was having was not as important as the validation of the encounters. The responses of the women became paramount to him. He tried very often "to stop and just be good." However, the interest of the woman nurtured his fragile ego.

The women he worked with became from time to time his sexual partners. His ideas about business and its goals were absolutely on point. He is intelligent and articulates clearly the proper direction for his staff. His issue driven behavior, however, created infighting among the women on his team. The pendulum of success swung from one extreme to another. When he left the company, his replacement was less capable but a more effective team leader. The "powers that be" felt that the company needed a less charming fellow. What the company's brain trust did not realize was that the women attracted to Donald were no less issue driven. There are women driven by the need to be with men who lead, men in charge, or out front. They have major internal challenges as well. Musicians, executives, ministers, athletes, etc. can all be the focus of these particular issue driven women. Their expectations are unrealistic; their pain is great and their un- diagnosed urges were compelling. After these "so-called" relationships are over many of these women feel hurt and used. Because of their denial, they never see their attraction (like a magnetic pull) to men who are emotionally unavailable. They continue to choose men with superficial differences and possessed the same core issues. Common belief is that opposites attract. The truth is, opposites attack, and likes attract. We tend to want who we are, that, that is complementing the issue driven agenda. In other words, we are attracted to those who help keep our issues active and intact. Two will not walk together unless they agree. A challenging dynamic for the reader may be in determining distinction. Is the responsibility of the players in this segment equal? Look at the people you like the most. We tend to forgive the people we like and hold others in our circle hostage to their unproductive behavior.

Donald became aware of his issues because of his therapy. He is on a course to recovery. As the manager, he was a powerful figure and is in charge at work. The women were aware of their attractions from the beginning, they were not forced or pressured to be with Donald. As life moved forward they believed (skewed perceptions) that each relationship it became the right one so they kept searching. The company may have only fixed half of the problem. The women are still there. Their perceptions are still skewed and the cycle continues.

Sadly many of the women who are attracted to the "Donalds" of this world never see their own culpability. The men they like or have been involved with could be a pastor, musician, married man, etc., for some women they walk away not seeing their own misgivings. Blaming Donald does not free them from the cancer of their own issues. Donald now manages with a greater sense of his weaknesses and a resolve to keep certain people at a safe distance. An older preacher from the south said to me one day, "The first time the dog bites you it is on the dog. The second time the dog bites you it is on you"

Chapter 13

Heather

Heather takes care of everything and everyone but herself.

H eather comes from a prominent family. A family filled with lawyers and successful upper-level executives. She has done well for herself. Successfully, she has climbed the corporate ladder never violating her moral values and sense of ethics. Heather does not lie or cheat. She is beautiful and could have almost anyone. However, she never recovered from the abuse at home when she was a child. Her mother was actually jealous of her beauty even at a very young age. The mother of Heather physically and emotionally abused her. Heather did not marry well. Her husband is emotionally unavailable and aloof. Heather is a tremendous manager and multitasker. She has not learned yet how to manage past her skewed perceptions of what it takes to have a successful relationship. She is one person at work and another at home. She is giving and considerate. Heather takes care of everything and everyone but herself. Her children will not see their dad loving their mom. Dad is not openly selfish however, he does not lend himself to validate or nurture Heather. Consequently, the children will have a damaged perception of a happy home and balanced parenting. Heather wants her children to be prosperous in their lives. She does not realize that she does not pick well in relationships; and that in part she shares the responsibility of her children not growing up in an emotionally healthy home. Additionally, heather is subconsciously teaching her children that they don't have to matter to their mates in the future. She is deluded by her material success for it provides them with palatial surroundings. Heather is not mean or aloof she is, however, issue driven.

Heather could become a greater parent herself by loving Heather. We should not justify or rationalize abuse, by others and ourselves. Take care of yourself.

Chapter 14

Sexual Intensity

When one lies and deceives their self into believing that, that is wrong is right, the end result is always chaotic.

The drive to be sexual is a complex issue. However, the topic needs addressing. To the extent of targeting one's lack of parental validation. Sex addicts as a child experienced various forms of abuse and an empty love tank (not being loved or nurtured by parents when they were young), this is the foundation of the sex addict or sexually driven. Sexually intense men and women are very often preoccupied with sexual thoughts. It is their way of connecting. In their heart of hearts, they believe that sex, or the lack of it is very often the reason that they are not as happy as they could be.

Very often men with a lack of appreciation for women tend to objectify them as beings of pleasure rather than people with feelings and needs. It may be hard to wrap your mind around this concept, but the fewer men care for women the more they have sex with them. The women and men involved in these so-called flings are just alike. Neediness not caring drives the behavior. They both enjoy being with people who are emotionally unavailable. Sexually driven people are incapable of emotional intimacy. The sexual activity of the issue driven is an attempt to anesthetize them from the pain of the emptiness that they feel. They are intensely sexual while being intensely lonely. Sex can never be a viable replacement for a meaningful relationship.

Theo is an extremely bright and perceptive man. He is liked tremendously by most and he is possessed with the ability to nurture and validate individuals around him. He is dysfunctional, however, and dysfunctional women with intelligence and substance are attracted to him. Theo never has one-night stands. Drawn to have sex with women that he has become friends with is his pattern. These women may be the wife of a friend or the sister of someone else that he has known well. Theo has left a trail of damaged connections. The women that were with him all knew that he was married. Many believed that they could have a better life if they could marry Theo. Theo often fantasized about being with these individuals in an endless loving relationship. It is the skewed thinking by both sides that keep the sexually intense going. However, they never see it as it is. The relationships never seem to work out. When the involvements come to a screeching halt some of the women because of their own denial and issue driven behavior believed that they were deceived. Issue driven humans very often refuse to accept responsibility for their unflattering actions.

Theo thrives off the validation he gets from being so effective sexually with his partners. He has never sustained an ongoing romantic relationship. The women in his church circle never see their own behavior as equally corrupt and reprehensible as Theo's. Some of the women became idiotic, driven by their irrational need for vindication and revenge. They became the center of dramas.

Allow me to explain. Theo was known as a potential lady's man. His marriage did not work. This is the norm for most people who have intimacy issues. They have no ability to maintain open and transparent commitments. On a few occasions, Theo was involved with different sets of sisters. The sisters knew that he was involved with their family members. To know that he was married, involved previously with another family member, and aware of the fact that he promises no future relationship; speaks of the damage and skewed thinking of the women. Additionally, he never made promises that he would leave his wife. My question for you to ponder is which or who has the greater issue. Is it Theo or the women who with eyes wide open preceded into the involvements?

Theo went for counseling and the counselor informed him that he was the weak one. The women he was attracted to were strong-willed and aware that there could be no future with Theo. Theo very often masked his own predisposition to become enthralled with beautiful women. He was in reality very needy. His low self-esteem pushed him into situations where other people with low self-esteem could not read the emotional cues. Theo tended to romanticize his thoughts of the perfect woman. All issue driven thinking is suspected it is nonsensical and appealing to other issue driven people.

All this being said the woman who was drawn toward Theo was in denial. It becomes too easy to deflect and blame other people for your choices. When one does this it is called issue driven.

Consider the dialogue between these issues driven individuals. With little or no transparency, what kind of connection could they really have? What would be the substance to the conversations? The platform of integrity has to be the basis of healthy relationships. When one lies and deceives their self into believing that, that is wrong is right, the end result is always chaotic.

Sexually intense people may never lose their sexual urges. However, it can be controlled and managed. The energy can be redirected into something productive. The sexually intense individual can learn that their partners are hurting and in pain. They can learn that objectifying people and reducing them to objects of pleasure is contrary to God's will and they will not be successful in relationships. Please note that there are countless people that have remained married for years and the extra marital affairs are quietly tolerated. This is not a successful home. It is an elongated marriage with unspoken pain. People with driving sexual urges need counseling and accountability. They very often try to be good and relapse.

Chapter 15

Communication

Some issue driven people cannot speak consistently in a validating manner because of skewed perceptions.

Issue driven relationships provide temporary relief and satisfaction. It is why there are so many people exchanging partners. These relationships are not reality-based. Issue driven people have fear and are hard-pressed to come clean in their communication with others. Trust is almost nonexistent among them.

A little-known fact is that issue driven people are hurting and in pain. What they often do is act out of their pain. We are very often judging the behavior of the issue driven as the problem. The real problem is very often buried deep inside the individual. In most cases they have no ability to communicate how they really feel, but only what they think. Again there is a difference between what they do versus what they are.

Within many families, there are systems of communication that are not conducive to harmonious living. Issue driven family members resort to idiotic statements, shame-based expressions (derogative actions and statements that put individuals down), and behavior that causes further damage to a family already torn by dysfunctional perceptions. If you let them, they will ruin your day. Issue driven people say things like "I feel like you don't like me." This is not necessarily the truth;

it is, however, how they may feel. Statements are very often repeated that challenge the worth and self-esteem of the family member. Those feelings are not true facts and they come from something deep inside the issue driven individual. Too often, these statements become tools of manipulation. Diverse feelings develop because of experiences that have affected the individual either negatively or otherwise. They may give a sense of being safe or not, and begin to develop a sense of self-worth or not as a consequence. Therefore, good or bad communication in families has a great impact on the self-worth of the developing members.

Some issue driven people cannot speak consistently in a validating manner because of skewed perceptions. Insecure people find it difficult to build the esteem of others because of their own depleted sense of worth. This truth, however, is not absolute because not every person filled with issues is the extreme case. The reader should work primarily on himself or herself and not look for issues under every rock. Emotionally healthy people seek balance. Balanced people communicate effectively. Issue driven people speak from their reality. The relational connection between person "A" who is emotional and person "B" who is primarily logical will be strained to say the least. The emotional person must understand that their feelings are real however, what they feel may not be real facts. The person driven by logic must understand that humans are not always logical. Their feelings and emotions are a part of the Divine construct. Sensitivity is not a bad thing for those who wish to be effective communicators.

Basically, the issue driven people are a hodgepodge of conflicting signals.

Jan is the mother of a family of two. The siblings grew up in a home where they developed all kinds of conflicting emotions and directions. The children were the product of an unfaithful father and a mother who retaliated by doing the same. Neither parent spoke in enduring ways to either child. Both children possessed above-average intelligence. Academically they were advanced but emotionally they were stunted in their relational abilities.

Jan and her sister were molested by a lover of her mother. Jan grew up with bitterness towards her mother for not protecting her from her mother's friend. Jan married again and her second husband molested her daughter. Jan was a committed provider for her children however, emotionally she was unavailable. Her education enabled her to climb the corporate ladder to a moderate level of success. Her communication skills limited her climb for she was indirect in giving directions. At home, Jan was no different. Her children developed tension between them because of Jan's way of handling conflict. The children very often perceived Jan as favoring the other sibling. Jan felt that she loved both her children. However, in her heart, she harbored a distaste for her daughter for being molested by her second husband.

In far too many instances of child molestation, the mother feels as though the daughter is competing for her man. This is simply skewed thinking resulting in poor communication. The tension between Jan and her daughter continued throughout their lives.

Communication is not just about vocabulary and language skill it mostly about what is in an individual's heart.

A good man brings good things out of the good stored up in his heart, and an evil man brings evil things out of the evil stored up in his heart. For the mouth speaks what the heart is full of (NIV) Luke 6:45

Chapter 16

Elisabeth

Magical thinking keeps her feeling safe and somewhat exalted; she is moored and harbored from the ocean of reality.

Elisabeth was born and raised in the Bible belt. There it was quiet and basic. Her dad molested Elizabeth when she was twelve. She had no conversation with her mother with regard to her father's violation of her. This is very often the norm in the events surrounding family boundary violations. As a result of having her boundaries damaged at an early age, she became promiscuous. She was a very pretty girl and male interest was not lacking. She later moved to a big city and experienced many men in her young adult life. She got pregnant early on and decided to marry the father of this child. This seemed like the right thing to do. The marriage lasted only a few months. Elizabeth never received counseling for the assault by her dad. Later she became a Christian and bought into a new ethic of morality. She married again. However, her new husband complained that his wife was frigid and lacked passion. Elizabeth developed a real sense of disinterest in her husband. Very often, she said things that hurt him and caused pain. She could not admit to herself or anyone that she really had become indifferent to her husband. The marriage was a disaster and the children of her second marriage grew up in a home filled with tension and despair. These children have a mixture of issues from both parents. Elizabeth is very controlling and continues to hide her hatred for men.

When she communicates, there is always an edge; she has underlying rage issues. One learns never to challenge Elizabeth about certain practices. She tends to be lofty and self-righteous in her dealings with people. Elizabeth can communicate rage and anger with the greatest of ease. Magical thinking keeps her feeling safe and somewhat exalted; she is moored and harbored from the ocean of reality.

I pause to reflect on the countless men and women who have come to me with similar backgrounds. If you were ever violated or abused please know that you were never responsible. Allow yourself to be forgiven. In some cases, you were too young to even know how inappropriate certain advances were. Some later have problems with separating the part of them that enjoyed the attention while hating the whole experience.

There is hope for you and help to full recovery. You are not alone even if you have feelings of isolation and alienation.

You no longer have to be trapped with your issues of hatred for the person that injured you. Hatred keeps you in the prison of shame and darkness "Vengeance is mine, I will repay".....(NET) Heb. 10:30

Elizabeth is a handful to deal with so she sometimes hurts others. The person who hurt Elizabeth was hurt too and perpetuated his pain on her. And so the wicked and ungodly cycle of pain continues. Hurt people hurt people.

No one ever dreams as a child to grow up and become troubled by issues. No one gets married to impregnate his or her children with self-sabotaging behaviors. However, it happens frequently with the issue driven. No sane individual dreams of becoming a problem and a nuisance to others, however, it happens. As a result, positive and effective communication among the issue driven is an uphill battle.

There are some who try to connect, they simply don't have the relational skill or character substance to advance the cause. Keep trying and stay positive for them and you.

However, there are others not given to peace and harmony. No matter what you do or try they love being difficult. You must protect yourself from them.

Don't let idiots ruin your day

Chapter 17

Issues can create idiocy

Bad or selfish behavior is the absolute choice of the idiot.

Idiocy is utterly senseless or foolish behavior; a stupid or foolish act and is devoid of appropriate protocols. The following is a list of "idiot" synonyms: *folly, senselessness, stupidity, absurdity, foolishness, foolhardiness, fatuity, abject silliness, inanity, asininity, insanity, madness, lunacy, utter rashness, suicide.*

Given the definition of idiocy, we must protect ourselves from the hurting and damaging practice of idiots. These issue driven people are unwilling to follow good advice. Without accountability, they will ruin your day. They will sabotage your life if you allow them.

Issue driven people make choices. They think and process information. They have free wills, therefore acts of unkindness and insensitivity cannot be viewed as mistakes and mishaps. Since their volatile acts are senseless and stupid, one must protect themselves by establishing boundaries. Bad or selfish behavior is the absolute choice of the idiot. Sympathy for idiocy is a waste of energy. I was taught that you could love bad people so much that they would change (I later found this to be untrue). Love is the weapon of heaven. This message was often repeated until, we as young Christians, believed in our circle that if we simply loved people they would change. However, heaven respects the boundary of choice. The Bible says (Revelation) "Behold

I stand at the door and knock if any should open, I will come in and have a meal." The key here is the will. It is codependent to think that by loving, you can force someone to change their will against their choice.

Times may be tough, circumstances may be unpleasant; however, you do not have to lie to get ahead or steal if you are hungry. A woman does not have to sell her body to get by. If someone has hurt you badly and you are furious, you don't have to retaliate, in the extreme kill them or threaten them. Idiots make choices dictated by their skewed reasoning. Their issues sired idiotic thoughts and absurd behavior followed. Beware for they will ruin your day.

William got angry while driving reached over and pushed Miriam his pregnant wife out of the car. She missed carried and forgave her husband. She later commented that she should not have made him so angry.

Susan was extremely jealous and insecure so she cut up the clothes of her husband and threw them out the window because he came home late.

George came home one Friday and picked a fight with his wife so that he would be justifiably angry. He left the house and gambled away his entire week's pay.

Chapter 18

What idiots do

They push for the disruption because of something inside of them that is off-line or tilted.

Idiots do not really enjoy peaceable and harmonious times because they are dysfunctional and issue driven. Emotionally speaking they have missing ingredients. They push for disruption because of something inside of them that is off-line or tilted. This is not to say that their intentions are always malicious or evil, but they could be. It may not be the direct intent to cause harm nevertheless the damage done is no less devastating. There are, as we have said earlier, individuals who choose to be unwise and practice senseless behavior. They support measures that are consistent with their own agendas, not necessarily what is in the best interest of everyone else. These people are very often peace breakers. In many cases, they would rather protect their **own** sense of well-being at the expense of peace and harmony in others.

Is there some safe place between heaven and hell? Is there some acceptable predisposition between the holy and unholy? If you are interested in this phenomenon, do a bible study on the biblical notion "a little leaven leavens the whole loaf." We Americans shun absolutes and extremes. The foolish that we speak of are idiots and are rightly labeled because of their choices. Only an idiot would make choices that will exclude themselves from eternal peace and tranquility. Heaven was too harmonious for Satan's preference. The order in heaven was proficient as well as efficient and the rejection of it created in Satan a chaotic desire that is so prevalent today. Everywhere he goes he disrupts and spawns discord. The Bible states if anyone lacks wisdom let him ask God. We see clearly that wisdom is available for all, not for a select few. Why would any normal or healthy being choose foolishness that leads to idiocy over wisdom that leads to relational harmony and a peaceful existence? The whys are beyond the scope of this writing, however, idiocy is the consequence. I am not leaving any middle ground. As Americans, we often seek the middle ground. A negotiated center where everyone involved can feel comfortable. Idiocy is not to be tolerated. Do you honestly believe that God would say "sin is not always bad, that he could live with some of it?" Remember Luke 12, the subject in the parable has the label, "fool." That label does not sound middle of the road to this writer.

Anyone who pursues a course that is instrumental in disturbing the peace and inviting havoc is issue driven. It is especially so when being involved in idiocy comes after receiving sound advice. The issue driven ignores warnings to avoid the hurting behavior and the destruction of others that will surely follow. This is precisely what idiots do. They do not regard the elements of truth that would protect others from their volatile actions and statements. It is full speed ahead for them. Again, perhaps they are not always malicious in their intent, but nonetheless, issue driven and dangerous.

Chapter 19

Thomas's story

Reality is not the friend of the issue driven.

Thomas is approaching middle age. He is married with children and lives in a home he cannot afford. He drives cars he cannot afford and he wonders why he can never catch up. I worked with Thomas trying with no success to help him with his core issues. He is a Christian possessed by magical thinking (he sees the world as he wants it to be not as it is). He is in denial about the true circumstances that comprise his life. Because of the low self-esteem that drives Thomas, he performs in church and other venues to receive validation. He and his wife both have dreams of fame and stardom so that they can live largely. They both are shallow (individuals caring more for external validation than internal quality) people. Thomas has an explosive temper and he is emotionally unavailable to his wife. Pressure came to bear and the skewed perceptions of reality convinced him to use money that was not his. Most of the people in his circle like him; and Thomas does whatever he can in order to keep his likable image intact. He lies to protect his reputation. When talking to Thomas you become aware of his choice to work only on the external. He would rather be seen reading a book that will help; than to actually get help. He will go to church but he is not committed to anything but the maintenance of his image. Thomas is issue driven. He may even be a bit narcissistic. Stealing and using someone else's money is idiotic. The law will prosecute Thomas. Yet he maintains that things just have not worked out for him. The fact that Thomas is a thief eludes him. Issue driven people never really focus on the pertinent facts. Reality is not the friend of the issue driven. Because they do not do reality, they may ruin your day.

The story of Thomas is complicated more by his support system. It was stated earlier that two could not be friends or walk together unless they agree. The people in his circle believe him to be different than he actually is. Thomas's accountability is those people who are codependent on him. We should constantly keep in mind that there is my reality, your reality, and finally the reality. It is tragic when people argue from their perspective realities and not the reality. Issue driven idiots would rather fight than switch. Their idiocy keeps them at odds with eternal truths. One cannot argue reality to an idiot. The idiot needs a change of heart. This will be difficult when the world around the idiot helps him or her feel normal or okay. The bible states "speak the truth in love." Idiots surrounded by idiots are like the blind leading the blind.

Ponder this notion that there are tons of idiots surrounded by idiots making other idiots feel normal.

Chapter 20

Raging idiots

These people become a horror to tranquility and peace. They feel no guilt and often no remorse behind their acting out, they have feelings of being threatened.

Anger is a strong emotion; a genuine feeling directed toward a person, an occurrence, circumstance, etc. Most people get angry. Anger is a healthy way of releasing steam. Some individuals are angry all the time. People with those issues tend to belittle and criticize others. Another type of individual who may struggle with anger is those who are sarcastic, practice-protracted grief, and suffer some form of continuous depression. Others have taken anger to another level. Some people, embrace a self-rationalizing rage. Their anger is something that is not easy to handle. They are out of control. It is their choice not to do something constructive to better themselves. Those who act this way tend to harm the people around them. This particular damage can be emotional or physical. They hurt their own chances of successful relationships. They may want more but very often get less.

If one should search the internet for a therapist there, Kate Barcus Miller, M.A writes:

Paranoid Anger: *This type of anger occurs when someone feels irrationally threatened by others. They seek aggression everywhere. They believe people want to take what is theirs. They expect others will attack* *them physically or verbally. Because of this belief, they spend much time jealously guarding and defending what they think is theirs - the love of a partner (real or imagined), their money, or their valuables. People with Paranoid anger give their anger away. They think everybody else is angry instead of acknowledging their own rage. They have found a way to get angry without guilt. Their anger is disguised as self-protection. It is expensive, though. They are insecure and trust nobody. They have poor judgment because they confuse their own feelings with those of others. They see their own anger in the eyes and words of their friends, mates, and co-workers. This leaves them (and everyone around them) confused*

Shame-Based Anger: *People who need a lot of attention or are very sensitive to criticism often develop this style of anger. The slightest criticism sets off their own shame. Unfortunately, they don't like themselves very much. They feel worthless, not good enough, broken, and unlovable. So, when someone ignores them or says something negative, they take it as proof that the other person dislikes them as much as they dislike themselves. But that makes them really angry, so they lash out. They think, "You made me feel awful, so I'm going to hurt you back." They get rid of their shame by blaming, criticizing, and ridiculing others. Their anger helps them get revenge against anybody they think shamed them. They avoid their own feelings of inadequacy by shaming others. Raging against others to hide shame doesn't work very well. They usually end up attacking the people they love. They continue to be oversensitive to insults because of their poor self-image. Their anger and loss of control only make them feel worse about themselves".*

These people are very often labeled rage-rs. Men or women can be dangerous to be around with rage issues. Wives, girlfriends, husbands, and boyfriends can be berated, threatened, or even physically abused. Children can have their entire future held hostage by men and women with issue driven rage. I know of women controlled by rage, they cut up their husband's clothes and tossed them out of a window. Many men now are serving time for assaults. A lawyer friend informed me that many innocent men are incarcerated and in the criminal system because of the rage (deliberate lies) of women. This is not an argument as to who can be worse men or women. It does not matter about gender, but issues and the behavior they drive. These people become a horror to tranquility and peace. They feel no guilt and often no remorse behind their acting out, they have feelings of being threatened. They will violate boundaries and think nothing of it in order to fulfill their issue driven need to react.

Raggers often see life through narcissistic eyes, seeing the world through its impact on them. In doing so, they become idiots. Just think about for a moment the atmosphere that their children live in. Because of the elements of narcissism in them, many are incapable of long-term caring and validation. Therefore, their children will grow up love-starved and shame-based.

Chapter 21

Franks Story

<u>Frank has never been able to see himself, it's always someone else's fault.</u>

Frank's mother was issue driven. She had a terrible temper and called the police to have Frank's father arrested because she was angry with him. She did and said many things in front of her only son. Her daughters will follow suit to varying degrees. She was shameless in her raging outbreaks; therefore, Frank and his sisters became shame-based. Frank has been fired from every job he's ever had; he never sees himself as the problem. Through a special program, Frank became a correctional officer. Frank's emotional predisposition could not take the verbal jabs leveled at him by the inmates. He exploded one day and now is facing aggravated assault charges for beating up an inmate. Frank feels like the other officers set him up. He often told his girlfriend that they had it in for him. Frank has never been able to see himself, it's always someone else's fault.

Frank's issues have caused him to be an idiot. A relationship with him will always lead to disaster unless Frank seeks help for his issues. He will ruin your day.

How often do we hear people say "I did not know that they were that way"? We are attracted to who and what we are. We are responsible for the relationships we have and maintain. Therefore we should not just look for healthy relationships, we should become healthy first.

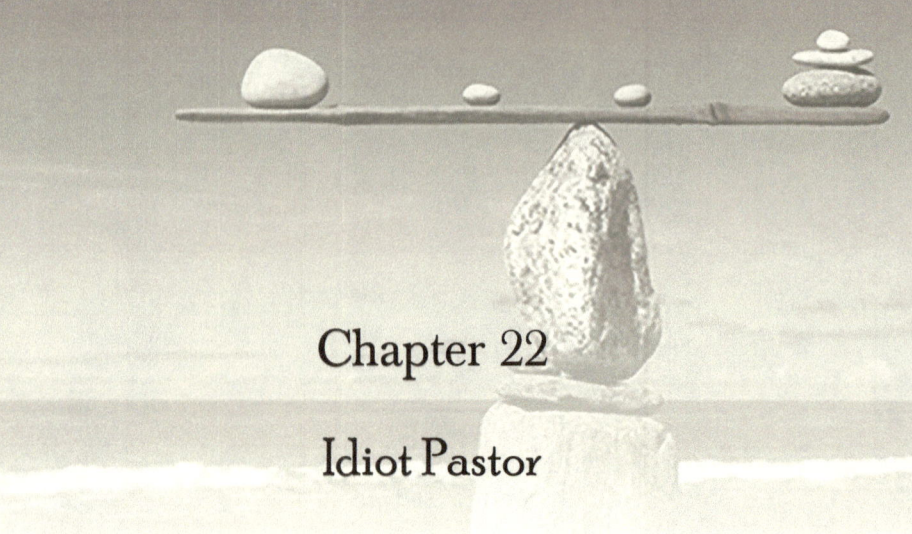

Chapter 22

Idiot Pastor

Legalism is a slightly veiled notion that you earn your way to heaven through good works and excellence in character.

Pastor Ron is a good man. He is moral and disciplined. He is a faithful husband and a great provider.

The foundation of his ministry is "legalistic". Legalism is a slightly veiled notion that you earn your way to heaven through good works and excellence in character. While these are noble qualities, the bible teaches that salvation is the direct result of the work of Christ on the cross. It is called the Grace of God.

If ever a person has a moral lapse in Pastor Ron's congregation there is an air of superiority coming from those who "never sin". Pastor Ron's life is the undeclared standard or model of Christian living in his circle. Scriptures are quoted and the bible is taught but there is a fear of displeasing Pastor Ron. If one does sin pastor Ron requires the individual to repent to God and pastor Ron for the indiscretion.

Any church that does not repeatedly teach and preach the grace of Jesus Christ as its curriculum –Vitae is a false church. Jesus is Lord and no self-proclaimed and self-righteous pastor is sanctioned by God to lead people in such a way.

It is the height of idiocy to remain in a church where a person is lifted up as God's example. We Christians are to seek guidance and instructions from God's word. The Bible plainly teaches that a connection with God comes through a relationship with Jesus, the Christ of God. No person ever becomes good enough to go to heaven through deeds and works. An eternal relationship with God is entirely based on the mercy and grace extended through the selfless act of Christ on the cross. Ten thousand days of good work and philanthropic behavior will never qualify any person for the rank and file that will populate heaven. God is not impressed with our improved humanity. He only wants to see from us a life submitted to the atoning power of the blood of Christ. To teach and preach anything else in the church is idiocy.

Fleecing people for their hard-earned money by telling them that they must give in order to get is a blatant lie. The Bible teaches the principle of stewardship or management. The resources that one has must be managed to the point of increase. Idiot preachers teach people to give and never mention save. Savings are a part of the Christian management protocols. The Bible teaches that it is for the parents to store up for the children.

Chapter 23

Biblically defined idiocy

It clearly says, "Fool." The word fool speaks volumes about the choices, character, motivation, and value of the individual.

Luke 12:20(KJV) But God said unto him, Thou fool, this night thy soul shall be required of thee: then whose shall those things be, which thou hast provided?

The individual in the parable is a prudent and worldly man. However, he has little or no concern, nor sense of the providence of God. He expresses no thoughts or notions about amending his current attitude. The uncertainties of life, the human drama with regard to God, the disposition of his soul, or the importance of eternity are simply words to him. Knowing this, how should such an individual be described? What word or words will be applicable to such a person? There seems to be common among many, a predisposition to downplay or remove the edge from some descriptive statements. When one must deal with matters as grave as the needs of the soul and its maintenance, are we only to use niceties? We lace our words with soothing generalities in hope that we do not offend. The ethic we employ when it comes to the grave matters of the soul is the question and its eternal resting place!

The word ethic speaks to a value, a moral precept, or conduct. While the word ethos means a spirit of a culture or sentiment that informs a belief. In a simpler sense, one speaks of the rule that governs while the other speaks to the motivation behind the spoken or stated rule.

The ethic of our American culture is pluralism, which means that there is more than one principle and that there may be more than one path to God. With this ethic, Americans tend to shun absolutes. This is what American coulter calls extremism. We chose less emphatic and categorical statements. The middle of the road approach becomes safer because it is more politically correct. Gone is the day when preachers declared holiness or hell. Preaching "hell" is too harsh and insensitive for our fragile and delicate American sensitivities. Churches that employ directness and forthright biblical principles that are not flattering will not grow quickly. We now rely on the powers of persuasion and imaginative catchphrases. Conditioned like Pavlov and his dog we only respond favorably to words that are soothing and palatable. Consequently, many churches are issue driven in that they cater to the American issue of indirectness. We must be proactive at all costs. Today people are not sinning they are just weak. They are not rebelling they have simply lost their way. People who drink and do drugs habitually are not drunks and addicts they are chemical abusers. Others who may act inconsistently with God's Word are only out of control and have lost the sense of them. Families that sire families who are dependent on welfare must be "spoken of" with political correctness. This is the new ethic driven by the ethos of "don't rock the boat baby." The translators of the NIV bible refused to have the word "sodomite" as is used in the KJV bible; God forbid we offend the homosexual community. Yet there are other considerations also where some are afraid to offend the heterosexual community that is active in their pre-marital sexual behavior.

There are times when God-given wisdom declares that we should be warm and charming especially when the saving of a soul is at stake for eternal salvation. There is nothing wrong with people who often need to be encouraged by kind and inspiring words. The prophet Isaiah said to "comfort my people." Can anyone argue against the truth of these words? Everyday life ambushes people. Circumstances crowd in on the believer just like everyone else. Words that provide a lift when one is down can be more valuable than hidden treasures. As stated in the book of Isaiah 50 verse 4 "The Lord GOD hath given me the tongue of the learned, that I should know how to speak a word in season to him that is weary." It is a mandate by God to do so. However, we must be careful, the instruction of the Sovereign is not intended to be a one size fits all proposition for every situation.

Let us look closely at the first half of verse 20 in Luke 12, "God said unto him, thou fool." This is not polite language. This writing is for all. The Holy Spirit does not attempt to cause the reader to feel warm and fuzzy. There is a message here and a theme that we should embrace. This divinely superintended statement recorded in Luke's gospel shouts loudly at us. The meaning is not obscured or camouflaged; you are not required to dig out its essence. It clearly says, "Fool." The word fool speaks volumes about the choices, character, motivation, and value of the individual.

The parable speaks of a character that is successful in his business venture. He was prudent and a wise merchant. He was a planner with the ability to implement to a favorable conclusion. His success proved to be overwhelming for his then current ability to house his massive production. How many American executives and merchants long to have these kinds of issues? The production he thought is moving so swiftly and proficiently that there is a greater need to increase my storage capacity (Wow! He was being too successful). The warehouses are not large enough to store the goods that we must sell; distribution will not be a problem. Some would call this the American dream. Yet there is a problem of monumental proportions. God considers man to be a fool. Is there a mistake or an error in God's judgment? The answer is categorically no! God can never be wrong. He is incapable of miscalculating, misstating, or misrepresenting. The natural question of most human beings is "why anyone with this kind of success should be considered a fool."

Too many humans have yet to embrace the principles of heaven. God continues to speak to us from His word, the bible. He urges us with his finger of love to seek first the kingdom of God. This rich farmer/manufacturer had misplaced priorities. His sacrifices have only been for the development of his earthly kingdom and natural well-being. This particular man has ignored all of God's urgings and requests by the Holy Spirit. God wants all born into this world to serve him and to make "loving God" our chief priority. How many still believe that what the Lord asks or requires of us is too much? After all, "we are only human" is the clarion call of the carnal and spiritually inept.

I have yet to describe what the main problem of the character in the parable in Luke. This person is not in this state because of circumstances. He was not pushed into this path because of a dysfunctional family. He could not blame his spiritual state on the local clergy and its inability. The real issue that irritated and aggravated his Sovereign was his foolishness, his idiocy. He consciously and deliberately chose the wrong path.

Webster states "idiots are those who are utterly senseless or behave foolishly."

I pose to you this question, "will a wise and all-knowing God send people to eternal damnation because of a mistake?" I think not. Sin is celestial treason and idiocy where Gods law is concerned. Sin is moral insanity and hell then becomes God's insane asylum. Those of you who read this may find the language too harsh. Perhaps some think that this particular style of communication is not in the best interest of human sensitivities. Others may accuse me of being crass or indelicate. My response to the criticism is a question "is the rejection of God and the notion of eternal damnation of the soul a small thing?" Do you really think that the Holy Spirit was concerned about being "labeled" rude when he directed Luke to record this parable? Are we not idiots when we waste our lives and strengths on that that only satisfies the natural man? What will we call the man that keeps all in exchange for his soul? Is this man simply weak, **or** will we say that he has only lost control? The ethos of rebellion will not allow many to take upon himself or herself the label of "idiot." I dare to refer to the written word of God, "Speak the truth in love." God is not being loveless when he labeled this man "fool" (idiot, utterly senseless and stupid").

Romans chapter 1 echoes these words in verse 19: *Because that which may be known of God is manifest in them; for God hath showed it unto them.* 20: *For the invisible things of him from the creation of the world are clearly seen, being understood by the things that are made, even his eternal power and Godhead; so that they are without excuse.*

I understand that many people have issues with God and his existence. Some would argue when did God become God? Did He make himself? God did not make himself! If God was to make himself where could or did He go to get the God parts?

How can someone or something exist in a building or make a relationship with them-self before they even existed? As a student of Philosophy, I find this position to be manifestly absurd. Only the Supreme Being qualifies for self-existence not self-creation. He has always been God! He is not one of us. Our design as humans is intelligent, wonderful, and proficient. It is the work of the Sovereign.

When you turn your back on God, you are an idiot.

Rom 1:18 For the wrath of God is revealed from heaven against all ungodliness and unrighteousness of men, who hold the truth in unrighteousness;

Rom 1:19 Because that which may be known of God is manifest in them; for God hath shewed it unto them.

Rom 1:20 For the invisible things of him from the creation of the world are clearly seen, being understood by the things that are made, even his eternal power and Godhead; so that they are without excuse.

Herein reveals the real problem/cause behind idiocy. The 18th verse states, "Who hold the truth in unrighteousness." People know what is right, they know what is required of them, and yet they willingly and stubbornly distort the truth and follow the untruth. In other words, they are being deceptive. Issue driven individuals guided by pride and strengthened by rebellion hold that truth is in untruth or unrighteousness. The pontifical arguments and rationalizations one might offer will not alter one bit the reality of God's truth.

Righteousness (goodness, morality, and purity) comes from faith in God, not in one's own means of self-preservation and distorted view of reality. After we have gathered all like-minded supporters, who are not willing to align themselves to heaven's priorities, we remain what we are, "idiots" if we do not repent. Thus, we have the notion of the blind leading the blind. Do not allow those blinded to reality to ruin your day or life.

Chapter 24

Where it Starts

Parents driven by issues tend to be disconnected and unavailable for nurturing and validation.

O ur childhood is a very fragile time in our lives. The best gift a parent can give a child is to love their mate in front of their children. Unfortunately, this is not always the case. Children that are raised in homes with tension and discord have become the norm in America. The selfishness of issue driven adults has become a pandemic. It is as the bible states "everything bringing forth after its own kind." Eighty percent of all children of alcoholic parents become alcoholics. As stated earlier, the same is true of children of divorced parents. Eighty percent of divorced homes produce adult children who will divorce. Issue driven parents reproduce issue driven children.

Children that grow up in chaotic homes tend to become adults with control issues, have addictive behaviors, and suffer from low self-esteem just to name a few. Adults who are emotionally unavailable were children raised by parents that did not nurture, or validate, and were emotionally unavailable. Children need desperately to be connected and to feel safe. Parents driven by issues tend to be disconnected and unavailable for nurturing and validation. Without these vital elements, children grow up filling the void with all manner of inappropriate means. Issue driven adults inappropriately model behavior for the children that they influence. Parents who experience no shame for their inappropriate behavior are shameless. Shameless parents produce shame-based children. These are people who can be guilt-ed into activities by causing them to feel shame.

In all likelihood, two parents who love God love each other, and love their child will produce children that will grow up with healthy attitudes. Real love is the answer. This sounds like a cliché. However, the Bible does not define love as a feeling or emotion. I state emphatically that love and loving is a choice. When you love you validate, nurture, and build the esteem of each other. The 13th chapter of 1st Corinthians is the biblical definition of Love. We learn through the teachings in this book that love does not keep records of wrongdoings and it does not hold grudges. We learn that love is kind and patient. Love does not act selfishly.

We must make a decision to do what is best for the object of our love. When I love you, I want what is best for you, not what I feel is best. The lover expends all to discover what the love-e needs (my emphasis). Love costs! It costs effort, energy, and many other intangibles. The greater the love the more it cost. God loved us by giving us his Son. The son loved us by giving up his life. We tend to love by giving whatever we can spare, hollow words, and a limited amount of ourselves. It is a small wonder why our children grow into people who care very little for others when they were not cared for properly by being nurtured and made to feel special. The lack of love produces more issue driven people than anyone can imagine.

We should not be ignorant with regard to the devices used by Satan and his army of demons. Issue driven idiots are without a doubt used by the evil adversary to ruin the days and lives of the people around them.

Children who would be healthy need to see love demonstrated in the home. The young ones need to view mom and dad first loving each other. How wonderful it would be for children to see often mom sitting in dad's lap and hurling kind words and gestures at each other. The children must be loved and taught to love each other. They also need to see love for offenders and sinful people. Real love is like the sun it shines on everything. The sun does not withhold its light on the less beautiful. Real love does not care about the worth of the object. Love lives to love and so should we. There are many unkind people in the world. Idiots are to be loved with boundaries. Tough love can be the only healthy course of action with regard to relationships with idiots. When children grow up seeing love with balance, they have a chance of becoming healthy. God does not give us permission to hate the idiotic. Only the contrary is true. We must learn to love them and not allow them to interrupt our lives.

Not only should children grow up seeing love in the home. They must first see the family system loving God. A loving family that honors God and His words as the true source of life produces less selfish children, who then become caring adults and parents. Worship and adoration to our heavenly father is the primary element of a stable home.

All of the individuals in all of the analogies given in this writing came from homes of origin that were dysfunctional. The stories are all true and the absence of unconditional love is real. This is where issue driven idiocy begins. People can go to church every Sunday and pray every day and still become issue driven. Dysfunctional behavior is sinful. The origin is a dysfunctional foundation started in the home.

Three valuable systems or institutions are defined in the Scriptures. (1) Romans 13 tells us about the State or government. Rulers are not a terror to good works. It is the government's job to imprison criminals and execute murderers. (2) Mathew 16 tells us that the church is to "go into all the world". The church's job is to build or populate the kingdom of God with believers. (3) Proverbs 22 tells us to train up a child. Basically, the home is an institution where values are taught, shown, and enforced. The home is critical for a society to become productive and considerate. I am oversimplifying but political ideology is the extension of the values learned from the influence of the homes of origin.

A man and his wife must consider before marriage the values they have with regard to raising a family. The Bible shares a notion of counting up the cost of doing diligence. An individual may care for a person and not like the way they will raise children. Couples should be on the same page with values that impact the development of offspring.

Earlier we mentioned Elizabeth. When she remarried her husband they had a different notion with regard to raising their son. Elizabeth was overprotective and would not allow the son to be disciplined by the father. Later in his adult life, the son asked the father: Dad, you knew you were right in trying to instill into me certain principles. Why then did you not fight harder to teach me because I became irresponsible? The father humbled by the question stated "you were right I should have I was in those days trying to pick the battles to be fought there were so many. Elizabeth and her husband produced children laden with issues. Not because they did not care. They simply did not know any better. The tension in the home was remarkable. There were constant arguments about money, sex, religious beliefs, and how the children should be raised. Neither knew nor could foresee the chaos that inundated their lives and offspring.

Chapter 25

Irresponsible Men/Controlling Women

Allowing someone else to speak against the tide of self-centered behavior will provoke growth in a positive direction. The real challenge is finding a life to model

I share these thoughts because of the negative impact the titled characters have on families, which in turn fosters issue driven people. Irresponsible men are very often but not always "mamas' boys."(Men who are perpetually tied to the apron string) Of course, they never see themselves as such. Controlling mothers help make irresponsible men. Women who dated and or married these guys (mama's boys) know exactly what I am saying. Some "gentlemen," I use the term with much sarcasm, are not mean and degenerate; they are simply big boys or babies. They never grew up. They have no real appreciation for what it takes to be the man of the house. Too often, their selfish agendas take priority over everything else. The women and children in their lives cannot rely on them emotionally. Perhaps they are not good at paying bills or providing leadership. They are comfortable delegating spiritual teaching to their wives. Their mothers ruined them. They are not producers but very often whiners. These men are always looking for a break, expecting women to defend them, or to make excuses and apologies for them. Some are good in athletic activities or have other special skills and talents but they are not a "man's man." Make no mistake they too are issue driven with all of the qualifying baggage. They have low self-esteem, tend to feel alienated, and have no internal sense of self-worth subsequently, no real sense of direction. They are absentee fathers even when in the home. They may lead immature women and children but they will never lead or inspire a group of men to constructive accomplishments. They are Mama Boys!

With accountability and transparency, they can find the path to wholeness. Allowing someone else to speak against the tide of their self-centered behavior will provoke growth in a positive direction. The real challenge is finding a life to model. Men should seek men to model after. A strong man can make strong men. Becoming a man of character is the goal.

Controlling women on the other hand like to see them as independent. Steven Covey states "three levels of human development they are: dependent, independent, and interdependent." The highest level is interdependent when one will say, "We can do it together." The independent states, "I need no one." Controlling women are not great team players. Many employ passive, aggressive behavior. The renowned sociologist John Bradshaw said once on a PBS telecast, "passive-aggressive is like a giant dog standing on hind legs in front of you, licking your face, and peeing on your shoes." Controlling women violate boundaries in the name of doing "good". They offer unsolicited advice. They are manipulative and they resent the label. Controlling women tend to be overly protective of their children and have no real emotional balance. Their acts of submission are contrived. These controlling women may push an individual to some relative greatness, but at a great price to the push-eel. Controlling women are strong-willed not strong women.

As uncomfortable as it is for the issue driven, they need truth spoken in love, accountability to a corrective process, and the willingness to fight their own self-destructive wills. Sometimes a church or religious system will employ a process of recovery consistent with its particular theology. Sad to say there is the existence of a theological belief system that may be counterproductive to emotional health and well-being.

Chapter 26

Issues and the Holy God

For sure only a heart in pursuit of the holy can love our Holy God

After reading this you now understand that there are people driven by issues and that their behavior can be invasive and boundary-violating. Idiots are people driven or controlled by issues. I talked to countless people in marriages, social situations, and strained relationships where issue driven behavior is the main disruptive element. The trail of wounded and disheartened people is the hallmark of those given to insensitivity. The selfish and self-absorbed have no time to be concerned with actions that cause others to bleed.

We read the bible and we see remarkable stories that speak of God's justice and judgment. We also appreciate that we as readers have committed injustices sometimes unknowingly and we may be possessed with issues that were troubling to others as well. This understanding begs the question; how does the Holy God deal with the notion of issue driven lives and others who violate and harm?

We read about punishment and judgment. Will issue driven people be punished and harmed for what they do to others? There is a biblical theology consistent with healthy and wholesome antidotes. The Bible is laced with healing principles that are balanced, effective, and relationally productive. We shall now explore the dynamics of a holy God and the behaviors of humans.

The idea of the justice of a holy God is a notion that arouses in us, feelings of ambivalence. As we consider this matter, many disturbing questions embrace us. What are the expectations of a Holy God? Upon what standard would this judgment be based or how will justice be dispensed? The idea of an absolute and non-repenting power passing judgment on us ignites within our being a tremendous sense of fear and anxiety. Understanding the justice of a holy God is an adventure that must be experienced. It is the hope of this writer that the questions asked and answered in this presentation will generate a predisposition that is essential for such a journey. That is a heart to search for an understanding of the holy. Further, we want to understand better that, that is not holy. This journey or pursuit is not primarily dependent on intellectual acumen. The spirit and the flesh are always at war. Every individual must say no to the loud clamoring of its flesh (outer system of non-spiritual reasoning) and seek the heart of God for this journey.

God's character and the definition of holiness are necessary components in developing an understanding of the justice of a holy God. There are questions that must be answered if the subject matter is to be properly developed. Can there be holiness without justice? How must a holy God deal with sin? Who can love a holy God? The discussion will take place that will examine human behavior in light of the holiness of God. Finally, we will explore whether or not God's wrath is justifiable with regard to sin or sinners.

I will not attempt within the limited scope of this paragraph to give an all-knowing explanation about the virtues of our Holy God. The unrecognizable, un-chartable, and inconceivable reasoning that is behind every decision made by our sovereign is too much to condense in this discourse. Nor will I attempt to defend the actions of our God whose insight and wisdom, defy the unlimited expanses of holy reasoning.

For sure only a heart in pursuit of the holy can love our Holy God

Chapter 27

Understanding His Character

All too often relationships with God have suffered because of improper representation.

R C Sproul writes in his book the Holiness of God "The mysterious character of God is contained in the Latin word "Augustus". To be august is to be awe-inspiring or awful. The study of the character of God will tend to hold us in awe while at the same time, it brings feelings of terror. God's nature speaks loudly of fairness and goodness. God's character is one of righteousness or right doing. The requirements that the eternal Father has for humanity and its treatment to others emanate from the core of his being, his character. Holiness is the pertinent element of God's being it sets the God of sacred scriptures apart from any other god. The God of the Holy Bible mandates through scriptures the necessity of understanding holiness. It was once said, "A reputation is what people think you are, your character is what you are". Unfortunately many only know God through the eyes of others. In a sense, they know Him only by reputation. All too often relationships with God have suffered because of improper representation. J I Packer writes in his book Knowing God, " *Those who know God have great thoughts of God. There is not space enough here to gather up all that the book of Daniel tells us about the wisdom, might, and truth of the great God who rules history and shows His sovereignty in acts of judgment and mercy towards individuals and nations according to His own pleasure. Suffice it to say that there is, perhaps, no more vivid or sustained presentation of the many-sided reality of God's sovereignty in the whole Bible.... Is this how we think of God? Is this the view of God, which our own praying expresses? Does this tremendous sense of His holy majesty, His moral perfection, and His gracious faithfulness keep us humble and dependent, awed and obedient, as it did Daniel? By this test, too, we may measure how much, or how little we know God".*

How well do we really know or understand the holy God? Are we interested in only His reputation and will we pursue a course that connects us with His character? Issue driven people are often stumped by this notion. What they know or understand about God is too often filtered through their skewed reality. The great tragedy is that those driven by issues need the help of the holy, but they reject not recognizing God's methodology. God's ways do not fit in to their logic of how things should be.

Chapter 28

Song of Degree

<u>Our humanity in the face of the holy is immediately traumatized at this clarion call.</u>

Much is spoken and preached about the love of God. In reality, little is mentioned or written of the holiness of God. In America, the song "Hail to the Chief" precedes the coming of the president. The protocol is one of pomp and circumstance. When the angels of our Lord sing the holiness of God (Isa 6) their song declares much more than the arrival of an elected official who may or may not serve the wishes of the people. There are recorded instances in scriptures (Isaiah 6, Revelation 4) when a man sees a vision of the throne room of heaven. These occasions were accompanied by the declarations of a select group of angels called "Seraphim". "Holy, holy, holy" is the singing pronouncement of the angels. R C Sproul writes in his book <u>The Holiness of God</u>, *"Only once in sacred Scriptures is an attribute of God elevated to the third degree. Only once is a characteristic of God mentioned three times in succession... it never says that God is love, love, love, or mercy, mercy, mercy. But it does say And one cried to another and said Holy, holy, holy, is the LORD of host: the whole earth is full of his glory (Isaiah 6:3 NIV)"*. Our humanity in the face of the holy is immediately traumatized by this clarion call. The angels assigned to the throne room of God are required to cover their faces in God's presence. They are given a special set of wings for that express purpose. Take a

70

moment and embrace this concept. When angels cannot freely look at God in all his Glory (Angels are sinless beings), it is understandable that humans like Isaiah the prophet trembled and collapsed at the sight of the holy. He literally came apart in the presence of absolute goodness and purity. He announced that he was "undone". Isaiah's traumatic event leads us to think, that God is both cause and effect, the object of dread and awe. God's holiness dictates that he is the stimulus and the respondent. Some humans often choose not to respond to the holiness of God. Especially those driven or controlled by certain issues, stating that they cannot be sure of Him or His requirements. However, the book of Romans states that "what can be known of God is manifest in them (in their humanity) therefore they are without excuse". The distinctive statement "holy, holy, holy" distinguishes God from any other being. This proclamation speaks about the quality that is the inherent nature of God. This quality (holiness) is revered and to be pursued by all (Lev.11: 44). It is the governing principle of His kingdom and the power of His will. It is the requirement for eternal residence in heaven. Finally, it is the method required by the Lord of creation for conducting our everyday lives. The Bible states, "For I am the LORD who brings you up out of the land of Egypt, to be your God. You shall therefore be holy, for I am holy" (Lev 11:45). Holiness is the theme song of morals perfection and sin is moral insanity.

Please do not confuse holy with religious protocol and accompanying pride in personal achievement. Isaiah was a good man but he was stunned and shaken by unmitigated holiness. Isaiah encountered an atmosphere of holiness that causes even sinless angels to cover up. The angels hid their faces from the sheer magnitude of the holy presence. Isaiah the prophet became challenged and recoiled. What I am suggesting is this. The remedy that is seldom offered to the issue driven is "having an encounter with God". God provides through his presence the fullness of joy. The presence of the holy causes individuals to see themselves compared to the holy, sinless, and perfect God. They Like Isaiah will cry "woe is me". Issue driven people tend to blame others and not look at their own stuff. However, the presence of God in an experience, a sermon, or a yielded life brings conviction. The issue driven who look into the healing light of God's holiness will cry woe is me. They will seek God's word for healing and restoration. The angels sang because of the intense presence and elevated degree of the holy moment. The "issue driven" who walk in their own way is just the opposite. Their complaining disposition is driven by their negativity. The "issue driven" do not seek with intensity the Holy, it is to them disconcerting.

Chapter 29

What is Holy

God's holiness is beyond descriptive abilities. He is transcendent

This is not a theological discourse it is an explanation of the character of our Healer. We all need healing.

Divine holiness defined as righteousness, absolute purity, and the absence of evil is not conclusive. God as it is stated has no ability to do wrong. He is inherently good. Every judgment and decree of God can only be good because of the absence of malice. Therefore, we can conclude that to say that God is unjust or unfair is to say that God is not holy. The infinite purity of God and His eternal righteousness are supreme elements of the divine character. However, this is the secondary meaning in defining the Holiness of God. The primary meaning of holiness is separate-ness, apart-ness, or other-ness. The otherness of God is underlined by His sacred difference. He is without equal in any manner (Deu.4: 39, Isa. 45:5, Acts 4:12). To say that God is "other," is to say that He transcends His entire creation. The Lord's Prayer teaches us that the name of God is to be hallowed. God's otherness requires that His name be venerated. We are not to take the Lord's name in vain. The Divine expectation for humans is that of reverence with sacred contemplation. The psalmist states *"enter into His gates with thanksgiving and into his courts with praise"* (Psa.100). God is to be approached with a sense of awe and cognizance of his splendor. Because of his apart-ness, thoughts of God cannot be defined in dimensional concepts. In other words, God cannot be described in terms of mass or density, height, or breath. There is no chart to measure His intelligence or device to evaluate His power. The Bible says in the book of Acts "In Him, we live and move and have our being". We exist because of Him. "God alone has the power of being," writes R.C. Sproul. We are dependent upon Him for existence. God on the other hand is self-existent. God is not delicate or fragile. He is inherently pure with an agenda that mirrors His ubiquitous divinity. However, the character of God is not only steeped in righteousness but also His ways and mannerisms set Him far apart from the mere creatures fashioned by His own hands.

The Holy Bible speaks of holy days, holy of holies, holy vessels, holy bread, etc. As we journey to understanding his character and explore His word we realize that only God can make something or someone holy. Any attempt to declare something or someone holy without God's approval is desecration. When God is involved or consents, it is consecration or sanctification (setting aside or setting apart unto God for God's service). Wow! God consecrates human desecrate.

The term/word holy is certainly expanded beyond the limits of morals and ethics. As you can see "Holy" as defined by people with limited understanding of God is finite. The colorful skills of the depiction of some ministers are still inadequate. God's holiness is beyond descriptive abilities. He is transcendent.

God Himself is defined, by God, Himself, for He is holy. He is other, He is God!

Chapter 30

Why Understand Holy?

We must understand Him that we are to love.

Since holiness is the true character and nature of God why then must humanity seek to understand it?

Isaiah the prophet was a good man. He was respected and admired. He was also of royal blood and privilege. However, in the presence of the "Holy", the sacred other, and unmitigated power, Isaiah became undone. He was traumatized by the presence and sense of absolute goodness. If a good man can feel uncomfortable and deeply challenged about himself what would an issue driven individual man or woman feel in that holy presence? With damaged perception, lack of knowledge or interest in the healthy, and diminished relational ability, what would he or she do in the presence of absolute goodness? An encounter with the holy will convict and challenge. The very essence of God will either draw one closer to God's righteousness or aggravate them to the point of spiritual rejection.

The world of unbelievers is comfortable with behaviors inconsistent with holy requirements. I find it amazing that the door posts of the temple responded to the presence of the holy in the book of Isaiah 6 and yet humans can remain unconvinced and unmoved. Perhaps God, who has been purported to be caring and kind, can be contented with knowing that a segment of humankind has acknowledged his existence. Some may even think that God would or should, be pleased with that kind of concession on his behalf. It is simply rhetorical nonsense. If God would or could accept such meager attempts at pleasing him, He would not be holy. The essence of God insists on worship, adoration, and departure from evil by His creation. In Psalms 19 we read, "The heavens declare the glory of God; and the firmament shows His handiwork. Day unto day utters speech, and night unto night reveals knowledge. There is no speech nor language where their voice is not heard". The elements of the universe bow before an almighty God. Mankind on the other hand is unconcerned and remains unconvinced about God's holiness. Reasoning supported by arrogance creates systems of belief that exclude the acknowledgment of God and his holiness from day-to-day living. While trampling over His commandments they ignore His plea for their salvation (deliverance from the power of the evil one). Humankind continues to celebrate their earthly accomplishments that create status among fellow humans they fail to recognize the standard of God. The standard, by which He measures acceptability, is God himself. Finally, God executes adjudication for such arrogance. Absolute holiness must manifest its distaste for evil. This expression is sometimes called wrath. It is Holy justice. The understanding of holiness is important because holiness is the nature of God, the object of our love. We are commanded by scripture to love the Lord with all of our hearts. We must understand Him that we are to love. To understand holiness is to understand God. To love holiness is to love the character of God. It is impossible to truly love someone and be ignorant of who they are. To know Him is to love Him. If we love God we are delighted to serve Him. Loving Him inspires us to be holy in all manner of conversation and activities. As we learn more about His holiness we become even more challenged to live holy lives. A holy person is a person who represents the character of God. They will never be perfect however, the heart of those who long for God hates the behaviors and actions contrary to God's will. They become less issue driven and become more like their Lord Jesus the Christ of God.

Individuals may speak kindly of their loved ones as a result of their experience with them. It would be terrible to see those to whom we relate often, only through the eyes of an outsider. The apostle Paul clearly demonstrated his hunger for more knowledge of his Lord, when he wrote " *that I might know Him in the power of His resurrection and the fellowship of His suffering*" (Phil 3:10). Not only does God require worshipers to extol him, He also requires them to be committed to His holiness (Lev.11: 44, 45, 19:2, Num.15: 40)

A group or sub-culture that practices a particular brand of holiness unique to that sub-culture defines cultural holiness. God has defined "The holiness of God" in sacred scriptures through human vessels. God invalidates the worship activities of individuals whose core being is not centered on biblical principles. The scriptures say "These people draweth nigh unto me with their mouth and honoureth me with their lips, but their heart is far from me" (Matt.15:8 kJ). Individuals who love to do injustice cannot be interested in a just and pure God. It is the effect of holiness. Humanity can be drawn to it or driven away by it. Issue driven people have a choice.

When we choose to understand the holy we then begin to hate the issues that create a behavior contrary to holy living. Issue driven behavior is in defiance of God's will.

Chapter 31

Justice

He is still just. God is not If God does not stop crime, He is still just, if He does not stop storms or diseases, obligated to operate within the human laws of logic.

Justice requires conformity to reason, correctness, lawfulness equitableness, and rightfulness. The natural question would be what system of reasoning or equitableness will God's justice conform to? Those who do not know God, or practice intimacy with him, take issue with the God who requires love and promises judgement for disobedience. This understanding in the minds of many justifies going away from such a god. Consequently, they believe in and worship other gods suitable to their own humanistic sensibilities, and palatable to their worldly developed tastes. This, however logical or rational is a flagrant violation of the holiness of God that requires the destruction of other images, thoughts, or creation of gods (Exodus 20:3). In addition, failure to comply will result with horrific and traumatizing consequences.

God is "just" in all His actions. He is fair if humans hurt other humans. God is consistent with his standard of treatment in vertical relations. He is not responsible for the pain caused by humans in horizontal involvements. Issue driven people may be very harmful, it is their choice and not God's duty to rob them of their selected behavior. If God does not stop crime, He is still just, if He does not stop storms or diseases, He is still just. God is not obligated to operate within the human laws of logic. Humans are often repulsed by God's actions in the Old Testament, yet they are indifferent to the suffering of Jesus for the sins of the world. This is typical of the inequitable perceptions of Justice by humans. Some would have you believe that the destruction of the Old Testament cities and their inhabitants was too severe. They shake their heads in dismay. Their expressed thoughts are wonderment and feelings of sorrow for the so-called innocent. These are simply misdirected emotions. God does not punish innocent human beings.

We must not look upon God's justice in terms of human fairness. We must always remember that God's justice is not decided by a system of logic derived from our limited brain capacity. Our souls are on trial. There will be no opposing attorneys fighting before a magistrate utilizing demonstrative tactics playing to a jury picked by our best efforts. Humankind's tendency is to always seek some kind of equitable solution that makes or brings balance to our fallible senses.

However, when we look at the cross in the New Testament, many are unaware of the concentrated punishment for the sins of the people of the world. We see in this event heart-wrenching devastation. At no time, in the history of the universe has there been a more severe act of violence than the wrath of God released on His son the Lord Jesus. Why! You may ask.

On the cross, Christ became a sin for sinners everywhere. The sin placed upon Christ while hanging on the cross was so repulsive that God Himself turned a loving eye away from His only begotten son. Isn't it ironic that the most devastating act of violence was poured out against the truly innocent in order that the truly guilty might be set free? Let me inject into the midst of my explanation a theological notion. "finitum non capax infinitum" is Latin and in English, it means the finite cannot grasp the infinite. The unbelieving world will not be able to embrace the kind of love that was demonstrated on the cross on our behalf. There are no cries for Jesus, and certainly no groundswell of sympathy. *"But He was wounded for our transgressions, He was bruised for our iniquities; the chastisement for our peace was upon Him, and by His stripes, we are healed"* (Isa.53: 5). The Lord Jesus literally took our place. This is grace in its purest form (treatment better than deserved).

No one has ever deserved grace or mercy from God. It is God's right alone to impart these gifts. If God chooses to give mercy, justice, has not been denied or delayed. If God decides to withhold mercy he is still just. The mercy of God is beyond being deserved, it will never be earned, and it can only be prompted by God himself and nothing outside of His holy being.

The justice of a holy God runs contrary to justice in the eyes of human beings. Only the spiritually uninformed would ask God for justice, on his or their own behalf. In thinking that they have been wronged, they fail to see just how much they have wronged God. There may be individuals, who have wronged us, and people that even misrepresent us, but never should we demand justice. God measures justice by a different standard. He most certainly will act justly, but are we sure that our lives line up with His just standards? I am glad for the mercies of God. Believe it or not, the "issue driven" as bad as they maybe are still breathing because of God's mercy.

Chapter 32

Conscience

As our inner man submits himself to the whim and will of God our conscience begins to reflect the light of his eternal truth.

Someone once described conscience as one's inner sense or motive propelling one to do what is right or acceptable. An inner value that may guide or direct....

With the moral revolution, some would argue that there are no absolutes. Relativism has become the guiding principle and reality changes often. This notion is a prevailing consideration in our society. However, God's word is static. The values set forth in the scriptures are enduring and eternal. The conscience of people can and will shift with societal norms. Conscience then becomes the expression of the desires of certain groups.

There will always be some articulate and persuasive individuals who will speak eloquently about the falseness or irrelevancy of biblical principles. They will tell us that we are evolving and that absolutes are a thing of the past. The issue driven people have corrupted consciences with regard to much of their behaviors. Thy experience very often no remorse or regret for actions taken.

The defense for Satan's lies and activities comes with a rationale that legitimizes human reasoning and lessens the culpability of our human responsibility. It simply has become a sign of the times.

Humanism rules it is the current philosophy of significance. With this paradigm, addicts are only chemically dependent. Rebellious children have simply lost their way. Sinners only need to find their selves.

Sin can and does erode the righteous status of the conscience. The key to understanding this is that the conscience must be developed and maintained. According to the Bible, the conscience can also be corrupted.

The church world has also fallen victim to the erosion of Godly values. The church accepts almost anything in the name of freedom and expression. Just because societal morals and ethics have slid in a different direction it does not mean that God's view and word have changed also. I run the risk of being labeled old fashion and out of touch. I by choice chose not to be in step with ungodliness. We, however; should fight to maintain an understanding of the pulse beat of the spirit. There is no other way to have a godly conscience.

What does a Holy God want other than holiness? As it was with Isaiah it should also be with us. Our hearts and spirit should long to bask in the presence of the holy of holies. As our inner man submits himself to the whim and will of God our conscience begins to reflect the light of his eternal truth. The reality of God becomes our reality it will govern us. We then become sensitive to actions and behaviors pleasing to our Sovereign. This is conscience. 1Ti 1:19 Holding faith, and a good conscience; which some having put away concerning faith have made shipwreck:

David in the scriptures was once a meek and gentle spirit. He would not even harm King Saul who was out to destroy him. However, after becoming king he with an eroded conscience not only took another man's wife, he engineered a cover-up that failed and then had the husband killed.

In Psalm 51 we read where the heart of King David was grieved with his sin. A heart or conscience that has seeds of God's word in it has the chance to recover. David cried "Create in me a clean heart and renew a right spirit".

Issue driven people must realign their conscience to the heart of God or others will suffer. People with issues that are unchecked and they are not in support groups or under accountability will hurt others. They will very often experience no bouts of conscience with regard to hurtful actions, statements, and behaviors.

Chapter 33

A Holy God and Sin

The standards of God's holiness will not be reduced for humans who are too rebellious, too busy, and too blind, to honor Him.

What is sin? Sin is a reprehensible action to the nature of God. Sin is a transgression of the law of God. R C Sproul writes *"the slightest sin is cosmic treason against the sovereignty of God"*. Sin is repugnant to God however, it is stated and presented; it is categorically repulsive to holy sensitivities. In the bible, we read, "the wages of sin is death". Every sin incurs a mortgage (a debt) that must be satisfied. Cash or time is not sufficient payment. The punishment or price for sin is death. Superficial acts of piety can never pay for the ransom of sin. A hundred years of doing good deeds will never be enough.

When God executes wrath (manifested justice) for sin, he is being fair. Every act of treason brings with it a death penalty. If a particular sin has been unpopular and then becomes popular, the penalty is not lessened. If it is wrong to sin for a penny it is also wrong to sin for a million. Whatever society's current view on sin is, it does not alter the realities of God's holiness. Human intelligence advocates a penalty system consistent with human considerations. The human predisposition is not inclined to contemplate holiness. Therefore, humans are not given permission to legislate righteousness. They are spiritually incapable of determining what is or is not acceptable to God. The standards of God's holiness will not be reduced for humans who are too rebellious, too busy, and too blind, to honor Him. This kind of behavior constitutes sin. God's penalty for sin is fixed. It is death! Sin can never co-exist with a holy God. The judgments placed upon sinful behavior and sinners are in order. Whatever humans feel about the system of God's justice it has no effect upon Him. Because God is holy, He is the declared enemy to sin and sinners, if they are unwilling to change.

In many ways issue driven behavior is sinful. Issue driven people very often refuse to love their selves. It is a sin to not love. Issue driven people can be judgmental and the bible warns us about judging. Issue driven people can be selfish, self-absorbed, and self-centered. The Bible teaches that we should deny ourselves.

We all sin! However, God has provided a means of freedom for us from the bondage of sin. The cross of Christ is the place where the ransom for our soul was paid. None of our self-proclaimed good works could ever be good enough to give us the right standing before God. The Holy God who hates sin has provided a means of escape and it was done as a favor. That favor we call grace. It is unearned and undeserved.

Chapter 34

Grace

Issue driven people very often misread the intent of God.

Those who study God's word in the bible understand unequivocally that God hates sin. Sin is a direct rebellion against the principles of holiness. Issue driven behavior is just one of many ways to violate God's law. The nature of the Holy cannot simply blink at sin. God is just in his judgment of sin and sinners.

In his mercy, God designed a system where Jesus the Christ of God would suffer the punishment for every person who ever sinned. Because sin is inherent in humans there is no one who does not need help from this wonderfully designed system. God is justified in his punishment of sin. He is also merciful in that His son Jesus took it upon himself to be punished for all the sins of humans.

A holy and righteous God must adjudicate wrath for sin. If God simply looked over or past sin he then could and would not be holy. As stated earlier the punishment of Jesus on the cross is without a question the most violent and horrific act of destruction ever perpetrated. Only with the innocent Jesus dying in the place of the guilty could the righteous requirement of God be satisfied. The penalty of death is the only payment for sin. If we were to pay for our sins how many deaths could we offer? How often could we die? Think if you will about the trauma of the cross. There was concentrated punishment for concentrated sin. Every sin that was ever committed by anyone had to be paid for or there could be no salvation. The sins taken on by Jesus caused the father to turn His head from His beloved son. In this divine transaction, the Father of heaven gave up his only begotten Son, for none other could have or would have given themselves for ransom. The Son gave his life he died willingly and sacrificially for the sins of the world.

The people of the church of Galatia were misinformed by individuals still loyal to the "mosaic law". Paul the apostle challenged them and asked them "why do you think that, that which was started by the spirit could be completed by the flesh"? Issue driven people very often misread the intent of God. They in turn create a religious system filled with duties, obligations, and challenges designed to satisfy the human ego.

Legalism is an issue. It is an aberration of the intent of God. Belief systems perpetuating such a notion are heretical. We cannot pay God by doing good deeds even if it seems noble. Guilt and shame-based sermons are normative in too many pulpits.

Grace on the other hand celebrates the unearned and undeserved kindness of the Holy God. Grace in its simplest form is treated better than deserved. When we operate out of a heart of graciousness we create no victims and we are aligned with the agenda of heaven.

The "issue driven", prompted by skewed perceptions never truly get it. They often make great attempts to satisfy the righteousness of God by extreme acts of piety, grandiose schemes of service while denying the principle of grace because of its simplicity. When one freely receives they freely give.

People of grace never seek for judgment. They never demand justice. We are all equally guilty before the Holy Sovereign. We have not only sinned but we are sinners by nature. Only an act of grace can transform us into acceptable vessels to God.

The theology of legalism has produced more failed ministries, damaged marriages, and members who feel they can never be good enough to go to heaven. Low self-esteem of those intimidated by legalism is a major is a major win for those used by Satan. The book of Isaiah tells us to comfort the people and to speak comfortably to them. Issue driven pastors repeatedly put people down to control them. Those churches are not a place of freedom but rather imprisonment.

Chapter 35

Moving forward

As you read this material some of you can relate and some parts you don't. My question to you is this. Is it beneath you to examine yourself and to see what is possibly there?

Do this:

- Ask God to help you discover biblically-based perspectives and behaviors. Read the scriptures daily.

- Observe with the help of an accountability partner the behaviors you have in question. Allow yourself to be challenged.

- Own your stuff. Don't deflect. Be honest about what your issues are.

- Prepare yourself for the pain of self-exposure. It does not feel good to have your raggedy ways and behaviors, published or out-ted. However, the people you may have injured are not having a party because of you. Remember the old cliché "no pain no gain".

- Take courage and journal your activities and thoughts. Make an effort to track your emotions and the triggers that inspire behaviors. Monitor the good and the not-so-good.

- Be realistic with your expectations. You will not get better overnight. In many cases, it took a lifetime to develop some of your very ugly behaviors. Be patient while you are getting better.

- Become a part of a support group where you can tell your story in safety. "Confess your faults ... that you may be healed"

- Testify and share your progress.

- Help others to see the light of an issueless life. Remain strengthened in your resolve to get better.

- Know this! God will perfect those things that concern you. It is God's will to move you forward into healthy thinking.

- Know that the journey in front of you is one of difficulty. But you can do all things through the help of Christ. Recovering is a part of God's design for you. It is God's purpose to give you the kingdom and live as a king's kid.

- Recovery is not an event it is a process.

When you make the decision to grow this will not be a happy time for all. Change is not always a happy thing for many. As you change you are causing others to change or adjust to the emerging person you are now becoming. This adjustment was forced upon them without their permission. It is a natural consequence of recovering.

May God grant you the wisdom to move forward, and may the light of God's truth illuminate your inner being so that your life can become productive and pleasant. My hope for you dear reader is that God's will be done in you.

Finally

I write this in hopes to raise the consciousness of issues and their impact on everyday living. Issues can be complex and diverse. This is not a book of antidotes, feel good material, or a cruel intention to create pain. I write this as a warning with concern for those who would be godly and emotionally healthy. Is it alright to harbor ill-will, cynicism, or bitterness over some past mistreatment from an idiotic individual?

Can we expect God to excuse us from a choice to not love or forgive? The answer is categorically and absolutely no!

I know Christians that raised children in a dysfunctional homes. The Bible speaks of everything brought forth after its own kind. The adult children of this particular household married dysfunctional people and perpetuated their illogical and erratic behavior. This family is comprised of general church workers. Many in that family system believe what they experience negatively is just a phase; they believe what they endure is natural. They are on their way to an understanding consistent with the logic of the issue driven. They blame others for the negative direction of their lives, broken relationships, and hopelessness. It is not remarkable that their issues affect their theology. Some identify this as "magical thinking." What about you?

References

King James Bible, NIV Bible

JI Packer Knowing God

R C Sproul Holiness of God

Aol.com

Vince Depasquale Starting Point

Elvin S Ezekiel Sr.

Pastor, Personal Coach, Church Growth Consultant

Elvin Ezekiel Ministries